A Matter of Life and Death

By Robert P. Sikking

DeVorss & Company, Publishers
P.O. Box 550
Marina del Rey, California 90291

IBSN: 0-87516-256-8

U.S. Library of Congress Catalog Number: 77-94991

Printed in the United States of America by
Book Graphics, Inc., Marina del Rey, California

CONTENTS

CHAPTER 1

A Philosophy of Life and Death

There is no subject on earth about which there are more spoken and unspoken questions than that of death. Our questions range from how the experience will feel when it comes our time, to why it is necessary for us to experience it at all. We wonder what lies beyond the experience, if in fact anything does. Does identity exist beyond death? Will we know and be known by our earthly loved ones or enemies beyond this experience? Can death be avoided, and if so, how?

As we consider these questions there is a myriad of other questions that come to mind. For most of us, the dilemma becomes so complex that we are finally willing to accept any philosophy about life and death that keeps us from having to wrestle with the frustration of not finding adequate answers. We even accept propositions that are irrational and unrealistic, concepts that are unreasonable and inconsistent with our other beliefs and knowledge in the other areas of our life.

One of the greatest reasons for all of the not knowing and the frustrations born of our ignorance of death and dying is that we can't seem to find a viable authority to consult. Most of our reasoning is amply supported by some authoritative body of knowledge or by those around us whose experience and expertise lend validity to our beliefs. Though there are those in our midst who believe or claim to believe that they have or can communicate with those who have passed through the experience of death, their credibility is questionable in the minds of the majority of people. It certainly is not the purpose of this work to question the validity of such claims, but rather to put forth a reasonable thesis, the very reasonableness of which can give a sense of peace and comfort and assurance until such time as proof can be obtained.

It is not possible, in light of the standards of judgment by which we arrive at knowing, to prove the ideas shared herein; therefore, logical reasonability is the criterion for this consideration. The Bible, which has traditionally been a source of information, inspiration, and comfort in regard to death and dying, admonishes us in these words, "Come now, and let us reason together, saith the Lord . . ."

The matter of death and dying is of great interest to most people and a reasonable, logical philosophy can be worked out that can make living our daily life more acceptable, more comfortable, and therefore, more productive. If our attention and our fears project our constructive thought power into the "never-never", we are involved in self-defeating activities that make to-day less joyous, less effective and less productive. In other words, the purpose of our existence is to *live*, not prepare for death!! It is my firm belief that if we can develop the right kind of attitude toward death and dying we can turn our attention to the more important matter of living life fully here and now.

In order to relegate the matter of death and dying to its appropriate place in the scheme of things, it is mandatory that we deal with the matter of life and living first. Here again, there are some pretty basic and fundamental questions that need to be considered first. What is life? What is the purpose of living? Why are we born in the first place? Do we really have control over our life, or are we merely pawns that are subject to the vagaries of fate or destiny? Are life and existence synonymous? If we seem simply to be existing, is there more to life and living that is eluding us?

As we enter together into this consideration, let us do so with an open mind and a receptive heart. At this point in our experience it is not possible to substantially prove any of the theories we may put forth, because as it has been facetiously said, "nobody sends post cards from the other side." The advantage of conceiving of a philosophy about death and dying will become clearer as we go along, because we will begin to release our fears, both conscious and unconscious, which for most of us are a very real force in our day-to-day living.

You see, most of the advances we make in the exploration of life are the products of a combination of conscious, reasoned knowing along with a not-too-specific spirit of positive expectation. We may never have climbed the specific hill in front of us, but based upon the many hills and plains and gullies that we have traversed in our life, and observed in the lives of fellow travelers around us, we have a philosophy about this journey. Specifically, we may not know what we will encounter and until we step out, there is no way to "prove" what is up ahead. Generally speaking, this is the sort of philosophy that has caused us to adventure into the unknown and discover the wonders that are all around us. It is not in the nature of man to stand still. There is a divine unrest that urges us on to even higher plateaus of experience, and it will not be denied.

The only thing that deters us in our relentless onward drive to the attainment of whatever good lies beyond us is the fear of the unknown. In the matter of life and death, the specific "blind spots" have proved, for many of us, a real detriment. There is enough knowing available to us, however, that will enable us to develop a philosophy that will allow us to push on. It will take a willingness and sufficient discipline to arrange our knowing in such a way as to accommodate the required positive expectancy or faith that will set us free from the paralyzing fears that beset so many of us.

Because of the "sense of separation" that is so much a part of the experience of death and dying as experienced by others, our fears of the unknown become grossly disproportionate and unreasonable. As we will see as we proceed in this consideration, it is a "sense" of separation, and not at all a separation that we have to deal with in the death of others and therefore in our own experience. A positive philosophy about life and death will make us wonder why we ever paused to doubt or fear. The progress that we can make in living life fully will be exciting and exhilarating, and the horizons to be conquered within our reasonable grasp.

The other side of the mountain beckons us with its inevitability. Wherever we are on the journey, on the plain, at the ascent of the mountain, on its steep and precipitous sides, in the meadows along the way, atop its summit or on the way into and through the valley beyond, we are still the same person, the same traveler, and not greatly altered by the changing scenery. The person that we are needs more of our attention in the creation of our philosophy of life and death than the experiences through which we pass. In the light of this truth, let us move on in this shared experience to know our self and encompass all of the wonders that lie ahead.

CHAPTER II

Our Death-Denying Culture

We in the American society specifically and the Western culture generally are basically a death-denying people. Those involved in research into death and dying are convinced that consciously and unconsciously we tend to deny the existence of death as a reality. Almost universally, we seek to shield one another from consideration of death wherever possible. Archie Bunker, a television character, believed in one episode, during a sojurn in the hospital, that he might die. In his attempts to give very bigoted directions to his wife, he was met with repeated refusal on her part to even think about death, let alone talk about it. Edith kept saying to Archie that she did not, in any way, want to discuss the matter. All over America viewers consciously and unconsciously related to Edith and to her emotional inability to face the possibility of death.

Much of our problem in dealing with death is not conscious. Since we were very small children the whole matter of death, much like that of sex, was just never discussed. Our parents and theirs before them felt that a child need not be exposed to the fact of death. Grandma or the elderly aunt who lived across town did not die. We were told she went to heaven to live with God. We were sent away to relatives while the elders did the necessary and mysterious things that were connected with the strange disappearance of that especially loved relative of ours. Though we couldn't understand the red eyes and tearful countenance of our family of adults, we exercised the only alternative that we had . . . our healthy, normal imagination. In the absence of any facts and any mature guidance from our elders, we were left to imagine all sorts of things. It is amazing how many erroneous conclusions a child can arrive at without the benefit of some mature guidance and some simple facts.

Much of our not knowing, produced by the fact that our culture tends to deny death, is quite simply internalized. The great gaps of not knowing quite naturally become irrational fears that can only be expressed emotionally. Recently, I was traveling in a car between Joliet and Chicago, Illinois. As we drove out of a small town into the rural countryside on a two-lane road, we were passed by an ambulance and a highway patrol car, sirens screaming and lights flashing. We were only moments behind the emergency vehicles in arrival at the scene of a very serious highway accident. It seemed to involve a semi-truck and trailer, an automobile and a motor bike. The truck driver was still pinned in the cab of his vehicle, the cyclist was lying dead nearby, and the occupants of the car were just being extricated from their vehicle.

I noticed a woman walking back from the scene of the accident to her car, which she obviously had left in order to see what had happened. She was clearly distraught, crying and shaking. Why does a perfect stranger respond in this way to death? An immediate defensive answer could be that the woman cares! Is it not conceivable, though, that we respond irrationally by way of our emotions because we can't help it? We can't help it because we have never dealt with death consciously and reasonably as a fact of life.

A staff member of mine once arrived at work in a very distressed state. She was ill enough to have thrown up on the way to the office. In inquiring the cause of the distress, this forty-two year old, educated, sophisticated woman said, "there was a terrible accident up the road and I had to drive right past the dead body of a man." What is it that creates such an abhorrence of a dead body? Because we have not rationally, reasonably and directly dealt with death, many of us have little, if any, control over our emotions when they are triggered by death . . . even of a stranger.

Much of our resistance in our society to hospitals and convalescent homes is said to be that they "reek of death." When a loved one is in the hospital, many people go through a clearly observable metamorphosis. Otherwise, we are very positive, "up", joyous kinds of people . . . until we walk into a hospital room. Naturally, we have concern for the wellbeing of our friend or loved one, but there seems to be much more to our response than just concern. We find that we have little to say and seem totally intimidated by the surroundings and the uniformed personnel all around. Often we simply withdraw within ourselves, but then some of us become hostile and belligerent in the face of this kind of experience. Nurses and orderlies in a hospital try to become enured to these changes in us, but it is not always easy. Fear of death and the emotions that it triggers in us need our rational, reasonable, and direct attention.

I have a very dear friend who, for his more than sixty years, has prided himself on his physical prowess. He has always been a veritable rock of strength and stability. He is intelligent and sensitive, strong and dependable. His pride in his physical well-being has always been totally justified. He has always been what my dad used to call "disgustingly healthy." Recently, he had a totally unnerving experience. All of a sudden one afternoon, he became disoriented. By that I mean that he began to reveal a forgetfulness of the activities of the morning and of the totally familiar circumstances of his home, in which he stood. Fear was not at all a familiar companion to my friend, yet here it was!! In exercise, he had wrenched his shoulder and all of a sudden it no longer hurt. What could all this mean? The more he struggled with this new adversary, the more he gave in to it. He spent several days in the hospital undergoing all sorts of tests. He had more x-rays in one morning than he had had in his entire lifetime.

The unspoken fear, the near panic that he experienced, is not unusual, except to him as an individual. How much more easily we could deal with the fear of possible death or imminent death if only we could externalize it! We are inhibited in our need to talk about death and thus to objectify it, because of our unreasonable, irrational fear of it, and because our society has made it difficult for us to admit to others the fear we experience.

Fear is as natural to us as thought. In our attempts to deal with it, we have attempted to hide it. This is an unfortunate fact about us and one that we must alter. Fear, when understood and controlled, is a very valuable asset. Fear is dangerous and destructive only when it is expressed solely or dominantly through our emotions. You see, there are two parts of us, an emotional part and a reasoning, thinking, intellectual part. It is when these two parts of us do not work together that we have difficulties. When the two of you or me work together in balance and harmony, we become the effective, efficient, capable person that we are meant to be.

I have a good healthy fear of falling, but it is seldom if ever expressed through my emotions. It keeps me from making silly mistakes in judgment and, as a result, I rarely ever fall and hurt myself. Each of us has many fears that are great blessings to us, simply because they are expressed in a balanced way through our thoughts and feelings. You see, when the two of us, the two of you, or the two of me are in agreement, in harmony, we are in charge.

When my friend returned home, he was given a clear bill of health. There were two great things he either learned or had the opportunity to learn. The first truth that he learned was that people care. If we are looking for the good in such an experience, the usual realization that people near and dear, as well as those strangers we need, do care, comes as a very strengthening surprise. My friend was moved to tears by the simple fact that caring is far more prevalent than most of us realize.

Secondly, my friend had the opportunity to learn that the primary characteristic of life is growth and change. Now, he may not have learned this truth any more than many of us have when we have seriously been forced to consider the possibility of death as an integral part of life. The lesson is there though and must be learned either by choice or by the force of circumstances. Death, as a part of the life experience, is a fact. We are going to have to deal with it sooner or later. Our objective should be to create a balance or harmony of rational, reasonable understanding with controlled, mature feelings in the form of a reasonable philosophy of life and death.

CHAPTER III

A Matter of Life and Living

In the establishment of our philosophy about death and dying it will be necessary for us to get a handle on life and living. The nature of life is that of change. Life is characterized by change. As we unfold in an orderly arrangement the knowing that is available to us regarding life and living, we will incorporate our positive expectancy or faith and a pattern will evolve. The pattern is already there . . . we will not be creating it . . . we will only be rediscovering it. What we refer to generally as life is merely a circumscribed expression of it. When we refer to life, we usually think in terms of a time span between birth and death. We think of it as "our life" or "his life" or "her life." What we must grasp at the outset is that this to which we refer as "our life" is only an expression, a part of life. Life is characterized by change, which takes the dual form of accumulation and distribution. Life is that activity in its multitudinous manifest forms that accomplishes a continuous process of "gathering together" and of "sending forth." It is that phenomenon that assures that there is nothing, absolutely nothing, that is truly static. Everything and everyone is in a constant and eternal process of change. Life is change. This being the case, there will never come the time when the process will not be extant. We are never going to arrive!

Now, this is a very subtle point that we need to incorporate in our thinking . . . that is, that we are never going to arrive, if by "arrive" we mean the attainment of a static state of perfection or fulfillment or completion. It is in the traveling that our purpose in life is fulfilled, not in the arrival at or completion of a goal. When we appear to "arrive" we have only come to another point of beginning. The limitation of time that we arbitrarily place on our living is an illusion. Life is! It is in no way circumscribed or limited by time. Time is a very relative concept that we use to endeavor to encompass with our finite thought, that unlimitedness of infinity. Time is a measure, a categorization of life that seems at the same time to assist in getting a handle on life and living and to limit us increasingly in doing so. Now, there is an enigma, if there ever was one! Yet that is what life is, in limited consciousness, an enigma. That is as it should be, because we are moving from spiritual near-sightedness to the attainment of a philosophy of the allness of life.

The "gathering together" or accumulative aspect of life is readily definable. As a part of life, two human bodies are joined in copulation and the sperm cells begin their arduous journey toward union with the ovum. The odds of any one single sperm cell getting to the ovum are hundreds of thousands to one against. The distance to be traveled and the obstacles to be overcome in an extremely hostile environment, the very strict limitations of time, make this union a miracle in itself. What propels the sperm? What causes the ovum at ovulation to make its journey to meet and join with the sperm? Life, of course! At conception, that point in time when the sperm and ovum are united, the thus impregnated ovum repels any other sperm and attaches itself to the interior wall of the womb and the life process moves on. The instant that the union is accomplished the ovum rejects all other attempts to make union on the part of other sperm. From within itself and from its environment, the fertile ovum begins to draw all that is necessary for the formation of a new being. Within the impregnated ovum there is a genetic pattern that has predetermined the sex, the ultimate size and shape and color and configuration of the new being.

A part of the wonder of the miracle of life is that it fulfills itself without the depletion of its environment. It draws together, it accumulates by virtue of multiplication, the very matter that is required to form vital organs, bone and tissue of body. The process seems so rapid, so sure, so remarkable. Before the conception occurred, the process of change that is life was going on. The "parts" that would this day be drawn together at conception were being irresistibly drawn to this point even before they could be defined as having an identity of their own. The life process cannot be limited as having a beginning or an ending.

Life goes on and the fetus takes shape, the marvel of multiplication moves toward that point, in the thing we call time, that is birth. Birth, obviously, is not the beginning of life, but rather it is the beginning of identity of life. "It is a boy," "it is twins." It is really life expressing itself according to a specific pattern. While this process has been going on at this point in time and space, it has been going on everywhere else according to other patterns. The mother of this child has buried tiny seeds from a packet in the prepared soil of her garden. They have seemingly "died" in the earth; they have begun the process of self germination and have come forth as tiny green shoots that have produced multi-colored flowers that will change into seeds once more that will again make possible the miracle process that is life. Never does the marigold seed produce a rose or a pickle, always after its own kind, a marigold.

As the conception and gestation has occurred in the body of the mother, as she has weeded her flower garden and enjoyed her spring display of flowers, the life process has gone on elsewhere that embraces these individuated expressions of life. The mighty pressures of time and tide, of wind and rain, have changed the form and shape of mountain and valley. Continents have moved imperceptibly closer together or farther apart. Astronomers assure us that solar systems and galaxies have moved on to alter the depths of space according to plan and pattern. Life is so much more than that tiny time space between birth and death. It cannot be isolated or separated into specifics, without producing confusion in our philosophy of life and living. Even if we, in our limited thought, isolate life in separate forms and shapes, it is not ever really isolated or separated. It is a part of the whole that is the life process of which all is a part.

While this "gathering together" process has been going on, all the while its counterpart, the distributive nature of life, has also been going on. The marigold fulfills its cycle of life, it wilts and dies and falls to earth to enable the process to go on. In the air and in the earth the process of disintegration occurs. The energy and substance that was defined as the marigold feeds the birds and the earthworms, mulches and aereates the soil and never stops being a part of the miracle of life. The grandparent or great-grandparent of the newborn child passes through the experience that we call death, having fulfilled in this physical form the cycle of life that has been identified as George or Sarah. Life doesn't stop or end, it simply alters its direction. It begins the process of disintegration that returns the energy and substance to the relatively unformed realm, that it might again be a part of the process of life that it has never really been separated from.

We speak blithely of the disintegrative process of life as "beginning" at that point in time that we term death, but in reality it has been occurring all the while. As the infant becomes the child and becomes the youth and becomes the adult and moves irresistibly toward the experience that we call death, it has been disintegrating all the while. The eliminative processes of the body have shed unneeded or unwanted substance with precise regularity. The individual cells of body and bone tissue have dropped away, having fulfilled their life cycle in the form in which they had held identity. The skin tissue has flaked away, the strands of hair have gotten trapped in the drain, the perspiration has dried and the measurable chemicals that it has carried out of the body have been blown or rubbed or washed away.

At the point of death, the body continues the process at an apparently hastened pace. The chemicals that for eighty or more years have functioned together in a balance that has conformed to a pattern that we have known or identified as George or Sarah now begin to react entirely differently. Each interacts with the other to hasten the process of disintegration. Either in a slow process in the bosom of the earth or a more rapid process in the retort of a crematorium, the form of the body goes on in change. Life is change and therefore, life is very much there in the midst of death and dying. These, life and death, are not as we have mistakenly believed, opposites, they are one and the same. Life is! We are life no matter our form or shape.

Death, then, as we have mistakenly understood it, really doesn't exist in the greater view. Webster's Dictionary defines death in part as "a permanent cessation of all vital functions: the end of life." The dictionary reflects what the majority of us who use the English language believe about a word. This that we believe about the word "death" cannot be true. To begin with, "permanent" is quite a definitive adjective and encompasses a long, long time! Life cannot end, though our definition of it as lying between birth and death certainly does. The greater perception of life as existing beyond our ordinary, limited notion, is a vital factor in evolving a healthy philosophy about death and dying.

If this broader view of life were not accurate, then death as being the cessation of life would have produced an inconceivable residue of "dead" leaves, plants, carcasses, and corpses never subject to change or alteration . . . and that just isn't true. But then, in spite of the clarity of the logic involved, death is a fact and the whole process of our effort here is to come to understand and deal with it.

CHAPTER IV

Disidentification With Death

Roberto Assagioli, M.D., a psychiatrist who lived and practiced in Florence, Italy, was, until his death, one of the leading research scientists in the study of the healing of the whole man. He was the founder and Chairman of the Psychosynthesis Research Foundation and author of an outstanding, exhaustive work entitled *Psychosynthesis* (The Viking Press). In this fine book, Dr. Assagioli presents what he termed a fundamental psychological principle: "We are dominated by everything with which our self becomes identified. We can dominate and control everything from which we disidentify ourselves."

He expands the principle by explaining: "In this principle lies the secret of our enslavement or of our liberty. Every time we 'identify' ourselves with a weakness, a fault, a fear or any personal emotion or drive, we limit and paralyze ourselves. Every time we admit 'I am discouraged' or 'I am irritated,' we become more and more dominated by depression or anger. We have accepted those limitations; we have ourselves put on our chains. If, instead, in the same situation we say, 'A wave of discouragement is *trying* to submerge me or an impulse of anger is *attempting* to overpower me,'

21

the situation is very different. Then, there are two forces confronting each other; on one side our vigilant self and on the other the discouragement or the anger. And the vigilant self does not submit to that invitation; it can objectively and critically survey those impulses of discouragement or anger; it can look for their origin, foresee their deleterious effects, and realize their unfoundedness. This is often sufficient to withstand an attack of such forces and win the battle."

Fear of death, when it becomes identified with our self, is a limiting, paralyzing factor and chains us to the limitations of separation that in truth do not exist. Now let us clearly understand that when we suggest that death does not exist as a reality we are not indicating that there is not the fact of death as experienced by hundreds of thousands of people every day. What we are endeavoring to do is see death in a new light, in a new understanding. There is the human physical experience in life, that which we call death, that is indeed a changing experience, but it does not involve, incorporate, or include any such thing as the cessation of life or the permanent separation from the life force.

So long as we continue to identify our self with the belief in, and therefore fear of, death as a permanent cessation of life, this will have dominance in our experience. We must, as Dr. Assagioli suggests, disidentify our self from the fear of any end of life. You may well ask how this can be done in light of the fact of the experience of death that we see on every hand. We can only do so if we can conceive of the truth that there is more to our individual identity than the physical form. There is more to you and me than bone, flesh, nerve and blood. We transcend our physical body. We are not our body . . . our body is something that we have. Your self has a body. My self has a body. The body that my self has and is functioning through on this plane of existence will undoubtedly pass through the physical experience that we call death. My self will, at that point in time, release dominion over this physical body so that the life process can continue to fulfill its purpose in the distribution of the energy and substance that have by that same life force been formed and identified over the years as me.

What is the self of me or the self of you? We are here suggesting that this self of us is not subject to death. What is there of us that transcends the experience that we call death? Everything about us that is physical is subject to the transitional experience that we know as death. It is reasonable then to state that the self of us is non-physical. The self of me is not Bob. That is just a human English nickname that I am known by. You see, I *have* a name. To people around me, that name is identified with my physical expression, and when I pass through the experience called death, people will say that Bob has died. My self, though, will not have ceased to exist. I don't know whether I will use the identification of Bob or not. I don't know, at this point in my evolution, whether I will even need such an identification or not.

In the religious world, the "I" of me, the self of me, is referred to as the soul. Webster defines soul as "an entity conceived as the essence, substance, animating principle or actuating cause of life, or of the individual life, especially of individual life manifested in thinking, willing and knowing. In many religions, it is regarded as immortal and separable from the body at death." The self of us, then, is the actuating cause of life. It is the self of us that has given direction to the life force in the form of us that has been identified as us by a name, a sex, a stature, etc. What is the soul made up of? Webster uses the word "essence," "substance," "animating principle" and "actuating cause" manifested in "thinking, willing and knowing." The soul is the sum total of the thoughts, feelings, intents, purposes, actions and reactions of us. It is all of the knowing and the not knowing that we have attained up to this point in time. Surely, then, the soul or self of us is a constantly unfolding, evolving entity.

It is reasonable to assume that this self of us, this soul is indeed immortal. In man's limited understanding, he has innately known that his soul is immortal, but because of his limited understanding he has had to give physical limitation to this immortality. He has conceived of other worlds to which this reality of him might pass at death. All civilizations of which we have any real awareness have had some concept of life after death. The funeral rites and that which remains of those rites, have given us insight into the beliefs of ancient peoples. Food, clothing, money, jewels, household objects, and even figurines to function as servants in the next world, have been placed in the tombs of ancient people. Our own Judeo-Christian concept of heaven and hell is an evidence of our belief in the immortality of the soul or self of us that transcends death.

In attempts to understand and communicate our understanding of life after death, we have had to struggle mightily to find words or symbols or phrases that are understandable. This has proved to be one of our greatest problems. How often we have said, "I just can't find words to describe what I feel or believe." In his most interesting book, *Life After Life* (Bantam Books), Raymond A. Moody, Jr., has recorded the stories related to him over a number of years by individuals who have had near-death experiences and those who have been clinically dead only to return to life and live to report their experience. The book cannot be considered "scientific" and the author so states this, but the striking similarities reported by those concerned leave little question as to the reality of life after life. Many of those sharing their experience did so for the first time to the author. In most instances, the person finds great difficulty in knowing how to express in human terms, words or symbols, the experience through which he has passed.

If we can, in the development of a constructive philosophy of life and death, come to disidentify our self with the concept of life and the concept of death, we may well be able to overcome this difficulty. We can do this if we can come to see that life, in the limited sense in which we use the word, is an experience that the self of us has. Man is. Life is something that he experiences. You are. You are eternal, you

always have been, you always will be, regardless of
the experiences that you have. Now, in the broader
sense of life as we have here been considering it,
you are life, I am life. The life that we experience,
though, is not something to which we are subject.
Instead, it is an experience that we have drawn to us
and over which we have dominion and authority, not
the other way around.

Stop now and think about that; it is a pretty staggering idea, one which we cannot prove or disprove.
Remember, the purpose of this exercise is to evolve
a philosophy regarding life and death that is reasonable enough to allow our faith to free us from doubt,
fear, and frustration, and to open the way for us to
live life more fully right where we are.

Disidentification is also necessary in regard to
death. Death is a human experience, like eating.
It is a part of the life experience. We do not die,
we simply pass through the experience of death. The
self of you, the self of me which is the real us, the
real you and the real me, is an eternal entity which
chooses to have certain experiences. We have chosen,
the real self of us, to have this experience that we
call life and we shall just as surely choose to go
through the experience that we call death because
it is a part of the life experience. Now that shouldn't
be difficult for us to deal with if we have grasped
the concept that death is not a cessation of life, but
rather it is an experience in life. We can disidentify
our self from the concept of cessation of life and
permanent dissolution of life by seeing this experience

for what it truly is. It is a transit on, it is a change, it is a movement . . . it is a part of life.

For centuries the idea of death has been considered to be the great enemy of man. Death is not an enemy; it is a part of life. If life is a valid, important and worthwhile experience, then death as a part of life is valid, important and worthwhile. Death, the cessation of life, has been considered the last enemy because Paul, in his letter to the Corinthians said, "The last enemy that shall be destroyed is death." Christian and non-Christian alike has accepted this sentence in such a negative way. Death shall not be destroyed, nor shall it be overcome. Death is a part of life, and surely one day we shall choose no longer to experience it; but it is not so significant that we should give it the power to be a matter that must be fought against.

For centuries, gravity was considered to be an enemy to man, because it kept us from experiencing the freedom of flight. Since we have subsequently discovered the laws governing flight, we know that if it weren't for gravity, we not only would not be able to fly, but we would not be able to stay on the earth. Gravity was never an enemy; it is simply a part of the three-dimensional life experience and as such, must be understood. We had to disidentify our self with the thought of gravity as an enemy. We must also disidentify our self from the thought of death as an enemy.

Disidentification of the self from the limited concept of death will occur, just like the disidentification of the self from the limited concept of gravity did, but there is no reason on earth why we cannot take steps to cause that to occur as an act of faith. If it is reasonable that death is part of life and not a thing to be feared, then it is within our grasp to utilize our confident expectancy, our faith, in such a way that our life experience can be altered to bring greater peace, joy, and effective living here and now.

It must be borne in mind that one will not simply be able to read these words and, as a result experience the disidentification; it will take time. We have spent a lifetime, influenced by the subtle pressure of the lifetimes of all with whom we have come in contact, learning to believe about death and dying from a negative standpoint. There will need to be a concerted effort over an extended period of time to come to truly live by this new philosophy of life regarding death and dying.

CHAPTER V

The Immortality of Man

As we have seen, our Judeo-Christian heritage has endowed us with a concept that gives evidence of our basic belief in the immortality of the soul. This concept is not original to our heritage, for we have ample evidence that the belief in a hereafter greatly antedates Judaism or Christianity. In some form or another, man has always believed that something had to succeed death. Our problem has always been that we have tried to fit a blind faith in a hereafter within the obvious limitations of our understanding. Because our limitation in consciousness could see only a three-dimensional universe, it was quite logical that we would formulate a three-dimensional hereafter.

It is safe to assume that over the ages of our development of understanding, we conceived first of a heaven as our hereafter. By heaven we must understand that whatever lay beyond death, it was first conceived of as good or better than our life experience here on earth. There is innate within man a basic optimism. We may very well have rationalized a negative or pessimistic attitude, but man's first impulse is positive, basically optimistic. Pessimism and negativity are learned attitudes. Children are instinctively positive, expectant and optimistic. They have to learn to be the opposite.

Intrinsically, man is positive and optimistic; extrinsically he has learned to doubt, fear, and expect something less than the best.

Because man has only been able to see or understand himself to be a physical being, living in a physical world, it was quite reasonable that he should conceive of a hereafter within the limitations of a three-dimensional, physical perspective. Man was able to recognize that he and those around him seemed to die. He was not able to perceive that there was any rhyme or reason to the death process, with the possible exception of the factor of time and age. Still there was and always has been the expectation that something, somewhere, had to succeed death.

Over eons of time, man perceived of a paradise-like realm to which he would ascend after death. His physical body was dressed and treated in the assumption that at some undesignated point in time he would return to claim it. Even in the earliest dawnings of fuzzy thinking, man perceived of himself as being something other than his body. The paradise-like realm, since it was obviously not here and now, had to be elsewhere. The physically unattainable realm reasonably had to be "out there" somewhere. Heaven, of course, is the word that we have used to designate that realm, and over the centuries of usage it has become also descriptive of space . . . outer space away from the discernable limitations of this planet earth. The root word from which comes the word "heaven" is "oranus" which literally means "expandable."

In man's limited understanding he had perceived of his heaven as a place of eternal bliss and harmony and peace. There every need is met and every protection provided. But it is still a place; that is, it contains all of the limitations of a place, with height and depth and breadth. It was conceived to be entered through "pearly gates" along "golden streets." Still with all of the limitations imposed by our lack of understanding, it was a promise of better things to come.

Over the ages we have also developed the concept of an alternative destination after death. As our judgment faculty of mind evolved, we perceived of the duality of man, good and evil. This evolution in thought is allegorically portrayed in Scripture as that portion of the story of the Garden of Eden in which original man partook of the fruit of the tree of the knowledge of good and evil. It was logical, therefore, to assume that there was a place to which the evil ones would go after death. It was hell or hades, and was seen to be a place of torment and agony, where eternal damnation was our lot.

The word "hades" was the name of an area outside of old Jerusalem where all that was unwanted or no longer needed was dumped and burned. It is not difficult to see how the groping mind of man would fantasize his hell as a place of constant or eternal fire and damnation. It is not difficult to understand how such a concept would be geographically located in the opposite direction from heaven, and be imagined to be somewhere in the bowels of the earth. Still, like heaven it was seen to be a three-dimensional place.

Now, the concept of heaven and hell, as it has been understood, cannot be proved to be true. By the very same token, it cannot be proved to be untrue. Let us remember that our purpose here is not to prove or disprove anything, but rather to develop a reasonable philosophy about life and death, but more particularly death, in appropriate perspective. The alternatives herein presented cannot be proved or disproved either.

Since, as we have seen, death is not an enemy but simply a part of life, is it not reasonable that the true self of us will indeed transcend death, but need not necessarily be limited by the three-dimensional world or realm by which we have been limited in thought throughout the ages? The concept of heaven and hell is perfectly reasonable when viewed from the three-dimensional perspective. If we are going to shatter this concept, as all limited concepts must be shattered in the light of broader insights, then we must be prepared to provide ourselves with an equally reasonable concept to take its place. To do this, we are going to have to be a bit "far out" in our reasonable rationalizing.

The immortal soul of us, the eternal self that we are, already transcends the three-dimensional realm. It doesn't have to be trained or qualified to see beyond the physical. It only has to see once more the reality of its unlimitedness and step out into its true, unchanging, everlasting place in infinity. Paul said, "For now we see in a mirror dimly, but then face to face. Now I know in part; than I shall understand fully, even as I have been fully understood." (I Cor. 13:12) His analogy is remarkable, for we are coming to see that we, too, have seen ourselves, our universe, and its experiences as "in a mirror dimly." We have seen but the reflection of our own limited concepts.

Then, when the light of spiritual insight is revealed, we shall see our true self "face to face" and shall understand as we have always been understood by what is true of us. Spiritual insight will be reasonable and perceptible by our reasoning nature.

The soul or real self of us doesn't go anywhere. It doesn't have to go to any other place. Surely it is not limited to time or space. At that point when death occurs, there must clearly be a point or period of readjustment when it steps free from the bondage of limitation by time and space. Perhaps it is something like the experience that we might have as travelers on a raft floating down a river. As we flow along on the surface of the river, we are able to look forward as far as the next bend and we are able to see back from whence we have come only as far as the last bend. If it were possible for us to be lifted straight up, higher and higher, our entire perspective would change. We would be able to see to the rapids or calm places that lie ahead or back to the narrows through which we have already passed.

We see life hemmed in by the banks on either side and the bends in front of and behind us. Maybe life, at this point in our experience, is full and free-flowing with lush beauty all around, or perhaps it could be likened to shallows and turbulence of white water with lurking perils just beneath the surface. Whatever our immediate personal experience, if we could be lifted up, we would see an entirely different perspective. It seems reasonable that the soul or self of us goes through a similar kind of experience at death, because it sees again a perspective that it has forgotten.

Among the experiences discussed by Raymond Moody in his book *Life After Life*, there are many very similar experiences shared that convey the idea of the self being lifted up and away from the physical drama of death going on in the wreck or on the operating table. In virtually all instances, it is a positive experience of the revelation of an entirely new perspective. In many of the experiences the self sought in vain to communicate a sense of assurance and comfort to the others involved in the drama.

Because of our limited notion of life and death, strongly supported by our misconception of heaven and hell, most of us brought up in the Judeo-Christian tradition have tended to deny death as a real and reasonable part of the total life experience. Perhaps we can be strengthened in the development of our reasonable philosophy about life and death by considering what others outside of our tradition have come to believe.

J. Bruce Long, Ph.D., in an essay in Elisabeth Kubler-Ross' book *Death, the Final Stage of Growth* (Prentice-Hall, Inc.), points out that both Hinduism and Buddhism stress the importance of a full acceptance of the fact of death by the individual if his life is to have a real sense of meaning. The truly purposeful life can come only to those who look upon death as an ever present ingredient in the life process. To be freed from fears and anxieties about death, the individual must learn to meet death "as a companion to life, in the spirit of rational and tranquil acceptance."

We may not be able to fully understand, let alone explain to another, the realization that we can experience regarding death and that which succeeds it. We can, however, relate it as a part of life in our evolving philosophy. Dogen, the famous 13th-century Zen master said, "We are being born and dying at every moment."

Since we cannot, and must not, endeavor to circumscribe the hereafter within the limitations of the three-dimensional realm, we are going to have to function here in a consciousness of faith in the goodness and appropriateness of just what lies beyond the bend on the river of life. Our expanding, evolving faith will strengthen us to relate ourselves expectantly to death, making us know that the next new phase of life's experience will be appropriate and orderly for where we are in the eternal evolutionary process.

This is one of the most important and significant exercises in our growth process, that of developing our faculty of faith in our part in the eternal life process. We must grow beyond the belief that there is anyone or anything outside of us that can bear any responsibility for our growth. Other things or other presences may point the way, but growth is an individual process, the burden of which and the joy of which cannot be denied to us or denied by us.

CHAPTER VI

An Alternative to Heaven and Hell

For the vast majority of us who were raised within the traditions of our Judeo-Christian heritage, a limited and limiting belief in heaven and hell as geographically locatable places to which we would be assigned at death, has made it difficult if not almost abhorrent to consider any other alternative possibilities. There are alternatives and they can substantially strengthen and support our reasonable philosophy of life and death. The alternatives cannot be proved or disproved, but as we have seen, neither can the more limited belief in heaven and hell.

The theory of reincarnation is certainly an alternative. To many people this theory is abhorrent, scary and confusing. Let us, in our search for a reasonable philosophy regarding life and death, approach this idea with an open mind and see if it can withstand our criterion of reasonability. First of all, let us clarify just what we mean by reincarnation. This is simply re-embodiment. It is the phenomenon of the re-entry of the soul or self into another physical body. It is not to be confused with the theory of the transmigration of the soul in which the soul or self might return in a different form such as an animal, bird, reptile, or member of the plant realm. Reincarnation is believed absolutely by many more people in the world than there are Christians and Jews.

If the body is but the vehicle for the soul or self of us and is, as we have seen, an extension of the real you or me, then there is reasonableness to the concept. If the soul of man transcends the body, if the self of you and me existed before this life experience and exists beyond it, then it is not difficult to conceive of a pattern or pathway that could incorporate the idea of reincarnation.

There are so many incidents shared by so many people whose credibility cannot easily be discredited, who have had strange experiences that cannot otherwise be explained. Many years ago, I read of an incident in a book on reincarnation that was said by the author to have been shared first hand by a reasonable, responsible person of stature. I can no longer recall where I read the story, or even whether I will adequately or accurately share it now, but it added a tremendous strength and validity to me in evolving a reasonable philosophy about life and death. The person who had the experience and shared it with the author was a substantial, professional man of upper middle age. As I recall, a special point was made by the author to indicate that this was a man of stability. For the sake of this sharing, let me call this dignified gentleman Laurence.

Laurence was walking along a street in a west coast city where he had resided for more than thirty years. He was hardly aware of a young woman with a small, bright two and a half or three year old child approaching him. As they neared one another the youngster broke away from his mother and ran to Laurence shouting "Daddy, daddy, where have you been, why didn't you come home?" Needless to say, the entire episode greatly embarrased the young mother who, quite naturally, tried to dissuade her young son. The child, however, would not be deterred. To Laurence, this was a most disquieting experience for reasons of his own. The young mother apologized rather profusely, explaining that the whole matter would be disturbing to the child's father as well.

Laurence gave his business card to the young mother and suggested that with her husband's approval and cooperation he would like to call upon them in their home and see if there would be a repeat reaction by the child in his own environment. After getting over the initial embarrassment, the parents of the child became rather intrigued and did call Laurence several days later. A meeting was arranged for him to visit in their home. On this occasion, the reaction was virtually the same on the part of the child. Laurence said that he wanted, nay, needed to share an experience of his own.

Many years earlier, Laurence had been very much in love with a servant girl in his wealthy home in Britain. His parents adamantly refused to hear of such a liaison and forbade him to see the girl. At the same time they discharged her from their employ. Laurence and the girl eloped by night and unknown to his parents, boarded a ship for Australia. There, in the outback of that vast land, a child was born to the young couple on their isolated cattle station which they had homesteaded. There was a great pioneer spirit in Laurence, but their life, though blissfully happy, was made more difficult by his young wife's illness and physical dependence upon him.

One day when his child was about three, Laurence was mending a fence on his developing cattle station several miles from the house that he and his bride had built. He was approached by two men on horseback who inquired if he was, in fact, Laurence, the runaway son of the wealthy British merchant. He said, of course, that he was and was immediately arrested for stealing money and possessions from his father. The officers refused to allow him to return to his family, but instead shackled him and drove him away to a port city. There he was boarded on a ship bound for Britain. After the passage of several years, he was able to return to Australia to his family. Upon arrival there, he was unable to find his wife and child, but found their humble home in shambles.

After a considerable search, he was able to piece together information that told a sad story. The ailing wife and child ultimately starved to death in their remote cabin and had been buried by a passerby. Laurence was heartbroken and chose not to stay in Australia or return to Britain. Instead, he moved on to the United States and here made his own fortune. Laurence never remarried nor did he ever return to his own family whom he quite naturally blamed for the tragedy.

Since first reading of this experience, which I choose to believe, I have always hoped that Laurence might have found great peace and strength from this salutary event in his life. It has meant a great deal to me, because like other similar experiences about which I have read or heard, it is a source of comfort in its supportive role of confirmation of the continuity of life.

From time to time, we hear or read about very young children who have most remarkable talents or gifts. The child who at four or five is able to play the violin or piano at a level of competency to qualify for concert work, is a case in point. Of course there are all kinds of other explanations that could account for such skills, but I choose to believe that such souls bring with them not only a remarkable aptitude for music, but a deep love and absorption in it that makes possible the development of such a talent or gift.

Frequently, as we have reasoned together here, we have reminded ourselves of the fact that none of our hypotheses regarding death can be proved, whether we agree with them or not. It leaves us with the freedom to choose what we believe as a rational, logical, and reasonable act. I choose to believe Laurence's story. I choose to believe in the pre-existence that could explain the child prodigy. Because I choose to believe, whether I can prove it or not, my philosophy of life and death that now includes this concept, makes it a lot easier to find a logical and reasonable explanation for other experiences that I observe in the world.

When I was in high school, our double garage had an apartment above it. My folks rented this to a number of individuals and small families over the years in which we lived in that home. For one brief period of time, a family consisting of a middle-aged couple and their three-year-old child lived there. The child was a most beautiful and remarkable youngster. His capacity to carry on an intelligent conversation with any adult was most unusual. He was what my mother referred to as "an old soul." The seeming tragedy was that his very unhappy parents couldn't care less. He was often left alone for many hours at a time and came to be very close to my mother. He always called her Mama Sue. He was rarely if ever fed regular meals and was allowed to sleep the night wherever he happened to fall asleep. It became very easy to love this little boy because of the utter disregard his parents seemed to show him. Often, in late afternoon, both of these unhappy, wrangling people would have passed out from too much to drink. The little boy was left to fend for himself.

One day, he crawled into his playpen and went into a deep coma. His mother called for help from mine and together they took him to a nearby hospital. There he died. A thorough autopsy revealed absolutely no known reason for his death. "How could God . . . if there is such a being . . . allow this to happen?" was the heart rending cry of his parents. There just had to be a reason for such an experience! In the light of our reasonable philosophy of life and death, is it not conceivable that this soul or self chose this particular environment in which to function in order to fulfill either or both of the reasons for which we live this life?

There has to be an orderly and logical reason for every experience that any or all of us has. This just has to be a basic postulate upon which we base our reasonable philosophy of life and death. We are inhabitants of a universe that is based upon principle. There is no such thing as chance or luck. Chance and principle cannot co-exist, no matter what the appearances to the contrary may be. We know we live in a universe that is governed by principle, for if we can discover one principle then it follows that that principle must fit into and with other principles that do not defile it. Mathematics is a principle, therefore there cannot be the chance that under certain other circumstances two times two will equal anything but four. Our job, then, is to discover the myriad of other principles . . . or the rest of the orderly principle that is life.

There are two reasons for existence . . . or perhaps more accurately there are two phases of the one reason for existence. Our reason for existence is to grow and to be a part of the growth process of others. We come into the life experience to learn that truth or those truths that we are ready to know, and to be part of the growth process of those whose lives are intertwined with ours. Is it not conceivable that this little boy came into the lives of these people, both to learn from the experience that they, in their unhappiness could afford him, and to be part of their learning experience as well? I know that this brief experience had a profound effect on the parents . . . both his and mine. It affected my life and may, in turn, through these pages affect yours.

Let us consider another example. How can we account for the experience of the mongoloid child? Apparently there is no known reason why healthy, normal parents can give birth to healthy, normal children and then have born to them a severely retarded child who is often followed by healthy, normal younger brothers or sisters. It cannot be chance. There must be a logical reason why children born with a severe handicap turn up where and with whom they do. If it were possible for us, like travelers on the flowing river, to be lifted up to a point where our perspective is not so limited, maybe we would see that each eternal soul is moving from experience to experience in a very logical and orderly way, and from each portion of the journey that soul learns through experience the growth lesson that he is ready to learn.

The first time in this life experience that I ever visited Louisville, Kentucky, I was sixteen years old. I had always thought of myself as being a very ordinary person, not given to having strange, mystical, or mysterious experiences. My host on that occasion took me by bus down to the river to visit some sort of fort. We had to walk the last several blocks and as we did so, I had a very eerie feeling that I had previously walked down that road before. It was such a strong and compelling feeling that I shared it with my friend.

We stopped and I tried to describe what we would find just around the corner. It was an entrance to an apartment house. There would be a glass panel door with narrow glass windows on either side. I felt certain that there would be a marquee out over the doorway with glass ornamentation hanging down from it. Inside the entrance there would be a small foyer with a marble tiled floor. Straight ahead a stairway would run directly up to the second floor and parallel to it on the right would be a hall running to the back of the building. I could clearly see a row of mailboxes set in the wall just to the right inside the front door.

We proceeded around the corner and I was filled with an excited tingling sensation of anticipation. We were confronted with what obviously was, in fact, an apartment building, but there was no marquee and though there were narrow tall windows on either side of the front door, it was a solid wood door. We went inside and there was the small foyer with the stair running straight up to the back and the hallway along the ground floor parallel. There was a worn carpet on the floor and instead of a row of mailboxes on the right, there was a door with a plaque on it that read, "Manager." It was a very strange sensation to just stand there in this place where I felt so familiar but which at the same time I knew in this life I had never visited.

Just then, an elderly man approached us down the hall. We engaged him in conversation and I asked when the marquee had been taken down. He looked at me rather strangely and told us that it just had to have been thirty or more years earlier. We were then joined by the manager who filled in the other gaps. Yes, there were marble tiles beneath the worn carpet and originally the mailboxes were where the door to her apartment/office was. They had subsequently been moved along under the stairway. At about that point, I remembered a rather ornate newel post ornament which was originally at the bottom of the bannister. I tried to describe it and the landlady took us to her apartment and showed it to us. Some fifteen years earlier, her handicapped husband had made a table lamp out of it!

I suppose that there could be other explanations for such a vivid experience. Somebody at some time in the intervening years has suggested that my mind could have unconsciously been attuned to the mind of another and I could have recorded the impressions then. I suppose that could be. I choose, however, to believe that this is simply another evidence of what I believe . . . that we have all lived before. Krishna in the Bhagavad Gita said, "Just as in this body the embodied (self) must pass through childhood, youth, and old age, so too (at death) will it assume another body; about this the wise man is not perplexed."

CHAPTER VII

Life Is Eternal

Surely one of the disquieting aspects of the theory of reincarnation is the implication of an unending series of life experiences. Many people find such a thought repugnant. Who wants to be tied to a cycle of birth and death only repeatedly to be followed by more of the same . . . life and death? I suppose one of the greatest dangers to be encountered in the process of the development of a reasonable philosophy of life and death is the tendency to lock ourselves into any specific concept without reserving the right to abandon such a concept in the light of increased or broader insights.

In the light of our limited understanding brought about by our three-dimensional insight, the concept of heaven and hell as geographically locatable places was perfectly reasonable. As the fallacy of that concept begins to reveal itself to us, we can see that reincarnation is a reasonable alternative. At this point, we could so easily make the mistake of locking ourselves into the acceptance of the concept of reincarnation and thus inhibit our growth process in just the same way as before. In order to avoid this, it seems reasonable to be open and receptive enough to accept that reincarnation is not the final or complete answer, but rather it is but a step along the way.

Perhaps without realizing it, we have accepted, and passed over very lightly, a most profound concept. We have incorporated in our thinking the concept that life is eternal and that as individuated expressions of life, the soul of us, the life that is identified as us, is in reality a part of infinity, without beginning or ending. Now let us be perfectly frank with ourselves—we haven't a clue what that means! Within the finite limitation of our thought process, we cannot fully embrace this concept any more than we can clearly or fully embrace the concept of the infinity of space. At some point in our fuzzy thinking about space, we must just leave it to faith that there will later on be some kind of revelation. This is necessary because the question, "what is beyond beyond?" can so easily become frightening. In the same way there is much of the concept of life being eternal that must just be taken on faith for now.

Having accepted the idea that life is eternal and our soul or self is part of that infinity, it doesn't seem logical or reasonable to assume that we are locked into an unending cycle of births and deaths. There just has to be a logical reason for this phenomenon. Is it not conceivable that the truth is that life is eternal and as a result of mankind's limited understanding of eternal life he has made necessary, for the time being, the concept of death or separation? Let us see if we can draw an analogy to clarify this point.

We are driving across country in our car. We have not made this journey before, but at setting out, we have defined our goal or objective. Let us say we are traveling from Kansas City west to Denver. The journey is important enough to us that whatever we meet along the way, we must get to Denver. We arrive in Topeka and there is a road block caused by a burst main and we are diverted by detour signposts around a circuitous route by way of some small towns north of Topeka. Eventually, we get back on our main highway and again make real progress toward Denver. Perhaps there is a landslide further west and then a bridge out. At each juncture, it becomes necessary for us to take a detour to get around the obstacle.

Man, in his limited understanding, has conceived of death as the only alternative to eternal life, which he hasn't yet been able to grasp as a reality. By his limited understanding, and therefore limited use or expression of the reality that is true, man makes it necessary to die . . . at least for the time being. Now this limited fact does not in any way alter the eternal truth of everlasting life. The necessity to die can be likened to the roadblocks along our way in the journey of life. The detour is reincarnation. One day we will eliminate the possibility of a burst main or a landslide or a bridge out, and then it won't be necessary to provide or find a detour around any obstacle. In our eternal growth process we will ultimately come to know and thus to experience the reality of eternal life that at this point we can only imagine.

Let us go back now to our earlier thinking and remind ourselves that death on the three-dimensional level is a very natural part of life. In the early days of motoring across the United States, before the time of interstate freeways, the burst main, the landslides and washed-out bridges were not all that uncommon. The wise, seasoned and courageous traveler was not deterred by the detours, no matter how far off the chosen main road they might take him. He knew that he must and would get to his destination in due course.

With the insight that life is eternal, whatever that means, we are wiser, and in the light of the concept that we have lived before (even if we have no recollection of it), we are in truth seasoned, but we must exercise our courage to push on toward our ultimate goal or destination. Now what is that destination? The very presentation of a destination seems to present an inconsistency in our reasonable philosophy of life and death. A destination or goal seems to imply an end or finish to our journey and that somehow doesn't fit in very well with the concept of eternal life.

A destination is not an end, it is but a new beginning point. We cannot know what lies beyond the point where we find ourselves except to the extent that we have accumulated from other journeys in life a certain reasonable expectancy of what lies ahead. Remember our earlier analogy of climbing the mountain? We may not know specifically what is over the rise in front of us, but we cannot be deterred in pressing on.

It takes a lot of courage to feel assured that good growth and learning lie ahead, but it certainly beats allowing ourselves to be filled with doubt and fear and uncertainty. We can choose to believe what we will. It seems perfectly logical, in the light of past experience, that we will be happier, more efficient and more productive travelers if we are filled with a conciousness of positive expectancy . . . even if we can't prove the basis for that expectancy at this point. "On the plains of hesitation bleach the bones of countless millions, who on the verge of victory, sat down to wait, and waiting died."

Let us not hesitate . . . let us move on in the assurance that life is a glorious experience and that ahead lies rich, productive and soul-satisfying growth in which we learn and learn and learn. "Beloved, now are we the sons of God, and it doth not appear what we shall be: but we know that, when he shall appear, we shall be like him; for we shall see him as he is" (I John 3:2—KJ)

CHAPTER VIII

An Alternative to Reincarnation?

There is yet another alternative to the limiting concept of heaven and hell. It is a bit far out too, but is worth considering as a reasonable concept if the theories of heaven-and-hell and of reincarnation are not readily acceptable. This concept deals with overlapping planes of consciousness. I am writing these words riding on an airplane between St. Louis, Missouri, and Chicago, Illinois. Seated next to me is a young man reading an Agatha Christie mystery novel. I have read the book; it is a good one. At this moment in time, though we are seated side by side, we are functioning on very different levels of consciousness. Seated across the aisle from us there is a woman talking very rapidly and loudly about the funeral of a loved one that she is traveling to Chicago to attend. She obviously, and rather painfully, is functioning on a very different plane of consciousness than either of us over here.

Think back, if you can, to the last time you attended a concert or watched a television play. At those times, because of who and what you are, there were certain things going on inside of you in response to the stimulation of the music or the drama. Take a little time to imagine the different sorts of people who may have been listening and watching with you. Because of who and what they were at that point in time, it is possible to imagine that they could have had entirely different things going on inside of them.

Just as an example, the play might have been about a broken marriage and perhaps that stranger seated beside you was going through a similar disruptive experience in his own life, and you are blessed with a very stable, happy marriage. Surely in this event there would be quite different things going on inside of each of you. Because of my personal experiences in combat during World War II, I have a very, very different reaction to war films than do my son or my daughters. It seems clear that, side by side, we have the ability to function on very different planes of consciousness. To each of us in a myriad of ways, the passing scenery of our day-to-day world is obviously as different as chalk and cheese.

In the light of the realization that we are not our body, but that rather, we are housed in, utilize, and function through our body, and recognizing that our eternal self or soul is not circumscribed by time or space, it seems quite conceivable that at the moment of death we simply slip into yet another plane of consciousness. I cannot be aware of just where this young man beside me is, nor if he thought about it would he be able to be aware of where I am right now. Intertwining and interlaced within, through, above, beneath, and all around us, there certainly could be many other planes of consciousness of which we are totally unaware. We know, even though we cannot detect it that there are all sorts of radio waves around us all the time. Unless we have a receiver that is tuned into the right frequencies, we cannot perceive that jumble of words or music or static. Nonetheless it is there.

Perhaps when we pass through the experience that we call death, we simply slip easily and freely into another plane of consciousness; and perhaps for a time we even retain an awareness of the plane of consciousness out of which we have slipped. That could be a very logical explanation for the inexplicable awareness of previous experiences of many children . . . before they forget. Perhaps that could explain the strikingly similar experiences of so many of those of us who have had near-death experiences or who have been clinically dead, only to return to this plane of consciousness that we mistakenly call life.

You see, once we realize that consciousness is not limited by or dependent upon our sensual, three-dimensional perspective, it seems logical and reasonable that there might very well be overlapping planes of consciousness right here. The problem that we seem to have in grasping this kind of concept is born of our unconscious and conscious belief in the senses and what they can report to us.

There is a photograph that has kept popping up at least during the past ten or twelve years. It is, I believe, a photograph of a melting snow drift. It simply appears to be dark spots on a white background. The first time I remember being shown it, I was asked what I saw. I turned and tipped it, trying to look at it from every angle, and still I couldn't see anything but dark spots on a white background. Then the shower said, "Can't you really see the face of Jesus right there?" I had to confess that I could not. After more showing, and more searching on my part, the suggestion was made that I quit looking at the dark spots and instead, look at the space in between. All of a sudden there it was—the three-quarter front view, the high cheek bone, the beard, the long hair. There was the face so very similar to an artist's concept of Jesus. In order to see it, though, you had to look at the spaces between the marks.

We are so busy looking at the evident "marks" on our picture of life that we simply continue to see time and space, physical limitation, describing "here" or "there." Every time we look at the picture of life, we see the same things and we consider anyone who sees anything else as being a bit weird or kookie. If we could quit looking at life the way we always have, perhaps we could conceive of an ever-present existence of many, many overlapping and interlacing planes of consciousness from which we have come and to which we will go when we pass through the life experience that we call death.

This concept seems to me to be utterly reasonable, and since I have no difficulty with the idea of reincarnation, it seems logical to me that these two concepts could easily not be alternatives, but rather two phases of the same very reasonable alternative for a belief in heaven and hell. Death, being a perfectly normal part of the life process, is that transitional point at which the eternal self of us moves out of this three-dimensional plane of existence into another plane. Clearly, for most of us this other plane or level of consciousness is not perceptible to our senses, but that shouldn't be reason enough to discard the possibility of its reality.

At the end of the spectrum, that point of transition into the three-dimensional plane which we call birth, poses some interesting questions. The most common one deals with the time factor when we are on another or in another plane of consciousness. The logical answer or solution to the question may not at first hearing seem very satisfying, but it seems to leave us with no reasonable alternative. There is no way to measure the time span on other planes of consciousness because we don't know whether time is a factor on any plane except here in the limited three-dimensional realm. Peter, in his epistle said, ". . . one day is with the Lord as a thousand years, and a thousand years as one day."

CHAPTER IX

Growth Beyond Grief

If you have had the opportunity to read, or otherwise be exposed to, professional consideration of the matter of death and dying, you have seen that a great deal of thought is given to the matter of grief. Psychiatrists, such as Elisabeth Kubler-Ross, seem to feel that the grief process needs to be understood and dealt with in order to allow the full benefit of the growth that can be ours through meeting death in the lives of others and intelligently preparing ourselves for meeting our own death. I would strongly urge everyone to read the several outstanding books written by Dr. Kubler-Ross as a result of her research and seminars on death and dying. She is, unquestionably, one of the leading authorities in the field.

Relatively little attention will be given here to the grief process, not because it is not a valid factor in the establishment of a reasonable philosophy regarding life and death, but because I sincerely believe that ultimately it will be seen to be a process that we can and must outgrow. In other words, we can, I firmly believe, grow to the point where we can accomplish the growth that the grief process affords us without having to experience the grief.

Grief is necessary so long as we dwell in a consciousness of separation. Let us recognize that we do, in fact, live in a consciousness of separation. It is going to take a tremendous amount of growth to free ourselves from that universal belief, but it can be done. It will never be accomplished, however, until some of us make an effort to do so. The consideration of this growth potential for me as I write these words, or for you as you read and respond to them, may be a step in the direction of attaining a degree of that freedom. How you or I will be able to handle the challenge of grief when we are next confronted with it, will depend to a great extent on the stability and rationality of our philosophy of life and death.

Before addressing ourselves to the factor of grief, let us consider that out of which it logically appears to come. It is our consciousness of separation that causes us to experience pain. If we were able to realize the fundamental truth that our self, the soul of us, is not limited by time or space, we could grow to a point of understanding that we cannot really be truly separated from *anybody, anything,* or *any place*.

Now, just saying that does not make it so. We have all sorts of patterns of thought that are the result of a sense of separation and a host of others that are dependent upon it. In one volume it would not be possible to endeavor to deal with all of them, since their characteristics will vary with us as individuals. We can, however, launch into a "stretching exercise" that may add much to our understanding as we individually deal with the idea of unity or oneness within our own thought. Let's not assume that we are going to arrive at any specific conclusions, but rather, let's just "stretch" together and see where it takes us.

I live in the middle west and I can go over to our nearby shopping center and push a shopping cart up and down the aisles of our supermarket. I can pass very close to dozens of people in the process of completing my shopping. I can stand in line awaiting my turn at the check-out stand and be close enough to many people to reach out and touch them. I can go on a lecture trip and be within fifty paces of hundreds of people at a time. I can return to my office and in the course of a day, I can be exposed in a nose-to-nose relationship with hundreds of other people. Regardless of this propinquity, I am infinitely closer to my mother or my son, both of whom live on the west coast. Standing in the line at the supermarket, I could reach out over my cart and touch the man or woman in line ahead of me, yet in spite of our physical nearness, I am infinitely closer to my dad who died several years ago. Isn't that true for you, too?

Because we experience physical separation from one another does not mean that we have to be burdened by a sense of separation. I spent some time years ago in a hellish battleground in the forest just outside of Haggenau in Alsace Lorraine in France, trying to make an army friend comfortable before I had to leave him to die. The kind of wounds that he sustained made it clear to me that without the possibility of almost immediate surgical aid, he could not possibly live. His spine had been severed, and he was clearly doing a tremendous amount of internal bleeding which could be seen through the gaping wound in his abdomen. We had little or no medical back-up on this operation and even if one of our all-too-few non-professional medics were to find him, he could only offer brief surcease from pain, and I had been able to provide that.

His name was Dell Guy, and as the years have passed, details about him as a person have faded in my memory. We were close in training and in combat, he serving as my assistant squad leader. We were close in a way that only combatants together can really understand and appreciate. I loved Dell dearly, though I could never have said it in just those words. I can no longer "see" his face in my memory, but Dell is closer to me than most of the people whom I pass in my day-to-day contacts with others.

It seems that we transcend separation where there is any degree of real interchange or involvement. We transcend separation where there has been some emotional involvement. The interesting thing is that we are capable, to a certain extent, of transcending the sense of separation where there is any real love. We transcend that sense, however, only after the fact and, it would seem, involuntarily. Because of the sense of separation, we feel our separations most acutely in relationship with those whom we love.

Now, obviously we have another incongruous state of affairs in this matter. It appears most difficult to overcome a sense of separation in our relationships based on conscious love; yet after the fact of death, we seem, to a marked degree, to be able to transcend that sense of separation. We don't seem to make any effort to do so, it just seems to happen involuntarily.

Would it be reasonble to assume that love has something to do with the overcoming of a sense of separation? Even though, on the physical plane, we experience most acutely a sense of separation in relationship to our loved ones, is it not conceivable that that very love has a good bit to do with our ultimate capacity to transcend the sense of separation?

Love has been said by some to be an idea of oneness, of unity. On the physical and human level, love is the power that unifies one with the object of his love. Love is a drawing power that unifies, and as such, it is reasonable that an understanding and expression of love gives us the capacity to be free from separateness. To do so, we are probably going to have to add a dimension to our love that is not always evident in many of us. Love cannot include the concept of possessiveness.

I am one of five children. We are four boys and a girl, and one by one it became our responsibility and our privilege to volunteer for duty in the armed forces. Three of us were in the U.S. Navy and two of us were in the U.S. Army. Ours was a popular war and we all went into the service eagerly, though of course with considerable trepidation. I suppose, being young, we did not give much consideration to the kind of effect this would have on our mother. As we began to write home about bombs falling all around the ship and mortar shells raining down near by, she began to function like any loving mother, experiencing concern for her children. The opportunity presented itself for her to seek the counsel of a spiritual counselor and teacher. His guidance was quite simple. "Don't burden those boys with your fear; love them enough to release them to grow through the experience that has come to them."

It takes a lot of love to release our dear ones in the understanding that we can never really be separated from them, but if we are to live life fully, we must do so. We may be separated physically by being on one continent and our loved one on another . . . or we can be physically separated by being on this three-dimensional plane while our loved one has passed to another.

Since the self or soul of me is not, in truth limited by time or space, then I am really one with my mother and my son out on the coast and with my dad and Dell, my army friend, on whatever other plane they may be. Now the consideration of this concept is obviously going to take a bit of "stretching" but the results may be very surprising to you. Take the time to carry such a concept to its obvious, and then on to its less obvious, conclusions. It might do wonders for your reasonable philosophy of life and death.

Now, let us go back to the product of a sense of separation . . . that of grief. What is grief and what effect does it have on us? *Grief* comes into English from the old French word meaning *heavy* or *grave*. It is defined as "emotional suffering caused by or as if by bereavement . . . an unfortunate outcome." According to authorities on death and dying, grief serves the very useful purpose of bringing us to a point of acceptance of death as a physical reality and of moving us beyond the point of change to motivation back into the lifestream. Grief serves to purge us out of the arrestation that the death of a loved one causes in us.

Because of our belief in the sense of separation, death seems to stun in bereavement those linked through love with the deceased. To a degree, the basic motivations to life and living life fully are arrested in confronting death. If we can come to confront death as a very natural part of life, in the understanding that we can never truly be separated from anything, anyone, or any place . . . especially anyone or anything or any place which we love, we have no need to grieve.

The second definition of the word *grief*, "an unfortunate outcome," has clear meaning, acceptable and understandable to all of us. But perhaps it could also mean that grief itself is "an unfortunate outcome" of our belief in a sense of separation as a reality. It seems reasonable that the enlightened mind and heart can accomplish the purpose of grief without having to suffer through it. If we are going to consider this, however, a word of caution is very much in order. There is obviously a great danger that we will, in the name of enlightenment, simply continue to deny death and repress the very natural feelings of grief.

Perhaps a rule of thumb for our own use would be to ask ourselves some very basic questions as we are called upon to meet death and conceivably the need of the purging experience of grief:

> Is it difficult to talk about death as it relates to a loved one?
>
> Do I have resistance to the need to deal visually and physically with the body of a dying or dead loved one?
>
> Am I plagued with the question of "why" regarding the death of a loved one?

If we can honestly answer any of these questions in the affirmative, then we have need for the healthy purging that grief can afford us. Now let's understand that if we can answer yes, there isn't something wrong with us; it is simply that we haven't as yet grasped fully the ideal of freedom from a sense of separation. As we have indicated earlier, this growth doesn't come simply from reading words about it. We are here in the process of the development of a reasonable philosophy of life and death, and at this point in our evolution we are "stretching" quite a distance!

CHAPTER X

Dealing With Death as an Idea

How valid is this evolving philosophy of life and death? Of course, the proof lies in the effectiveness with which we meet death in whatever form it comes. To begin with, it comes as an idea. If we can constructively and positively deal with it first as an idea, then when it comes into our life as a physical fact, we will be in a much better position to have a growing experience. With each growing experience that we have in dealing with death, we have the opportunity to approach our own death by living our life more fully, richly and joyously. As we give consideration to the idea of death, let us remember that the purpose of this exercise is not simply to prepare for death as an inevitability, but rather to free ourselves from the unreasonable fear of death in order to live life more abundantly and peacefully and happily.

We could so easily become negative and even morose in our thought of the inevitability of death and we should make every effort to avoid doing so. Life is an experience to be lived! It is that of ours that produces the opportunity to grow. Growth is that activity that is ours that gives us increasing degrees of dominion and authority over our life experience.

In our evolving, reasonable philosophy of life and death, it is the very reasonableness that gives it validity. It is reasonable to consider our self as being eternal and that growth in and of our self as being our purpose.

As children, you and I have grown physically and mentally by meeting life as it comes. We were prepared by life, and by those around us who had more conscious experience of life, to meet whatever came our way. Each experience, whether we handled it well or poorly, added to the dimensions of our being to better equip us for what lay ahead. Our responses to the adult world around us, play with other children, curiosity in the form of a desire to learn, prepared us for our initial experiences in school. Grammar school equipped us to enter junior high, and that readied us for high school and perhaps more advanced educational experience and for adult living.

We might very well have chosen at any point along the way not to grow into the next level, fearing the unknown that the higher level would hold; but our philosophy of life, mostly inherited from those around us, made it possible for us to push on. Our circumstances demanded that in some way we move on, and in relation to death, we are in the same position. We may very well choose to avoid dealing with death, but it is a fact, and sooner or later circumstances will demand our involvement.

All around us, there is the experience of death, and unless it is something that we are physically meeting, or vicariously meeting through a loved one or a friend, it is simply an idea. Let's learn to deal with the idea as an idea. Every day in the paper or on the radio or television we are exposed to the idea of death. Instead of cringing from it or making yourself think of something else, take advantage of the opportunity to make your evolving philosophy a practical reality for you now. When you heard that bit of news about those faceless people who died in that natural disaster or in that plane wreck or that border skirmish, how did you deal with it? When the relative of a friend or neighbor dies and he shares the fact with you, how do you handle it? When you read about the senator's fatal plane crash, what went through your mind? How did you feel about it? Do you function in a sense of fear that is demonstrated by reticence to give the matter any serious consideration?

If the reasonable philosophy of life and death that we are sharing here has any validity at all, then we have a beautiful opportunity to grow with those faceless ones, to benefit by a constructive and positive consideration of death as an integral part of life. Each time we can thus affirm our positive, reasonable philosophy of life and death, it will become more firmly incorporated into the very fabric of our being. It is up to us individually to create the consciousness of positive, constructive thought relating to death and dying. Remember that we have a lifetime of cultural thoughts that needs to be altered. It's not going to happen overnight or simply by the reading of a book or the sharing of another's thoughts. We have work to do in this area of our life, and every day we are provided with the opportunities to get on with it.

For most of us, the opportunity comes sooner or later to deal directly with the death of someone near and dear to us. In the light of our evolving philosophy of life and death, how shall we do so? Generally speaking, the opportunity will come in the death of a family member or friend who has lived a long life and whose death has not come as much of a surprise. Our philosophy surely should have given us a greater sense of poise and peace about it as we approach it; but even if we have worked a considerable amount in the evolving of our philosophy, and to a great extent have begun to free ourselves of the fear of death, the death of a loved one still stuns us. We may be able to consciously approach the death of a loved one faithfully, knowing that life is eternal and that this loved one is playing out the role in life that he or she has drawn. Still, it is not unusual for us to feel strong emotion about this person's departure from this life.

Go any day to an airport and watch the departures and arrivals of several flights. You will see the expression of emotion that comes of a sense of separation, even for a brief, definable period of time. You will see the great joy that is expressed when a loved one returns from even a short journey. We would not want our philosophy of life and death to rob us of the beauty that is to be found in loving and close human relationships. They are truly wonderful. There is a depth of emotion that is hard to define at the loss of a loved one in death. The privilege of having become enough a part of another to deeply feel his or her presence or absence is one of the most beautiful experiences that man is heir to in this life.

Of course, at the outset, we should find from our evolving philosophy of life and death that even though we may use the words, "loss of a loved one in death," there is in truth no real or eternal loss. We can never lose that to which we have given the fabric of our love. There can never be loss in a relationship where we have been made whole and meaningful and purposeful by the mutual expression of love. Yet we may not, at this point in our evolution, be able to discuss at length the pending death of this loved one; and the person meeting this experience may not be able to discuss the pending event with us.

Perhaps the only, and greatest, blessing that we can give to a dying one is the aura of our unspoken faith that all is well, even if we cannot explain it. That kind of consciousness can be developed by us in the exercise of dealing with death as an idea, and as a physical fact in the life of this loved one. The limited amount of research that has been done in the consideration of death by those terminally ill has proved that each one is seeking to find meaning and purpose in this experience, just as in all other experiences of life. Perhaps you will be blessed with the opportunity to seek meaning and purpose along with the loved one as he or she seeks it in this exprience.

Your loved one is not somehow a different being simply because he or she is meeting this particular experience in life. Don't change your demeanor, don't get all pious and serious, unless that is your nature normally in relationship to this loved one. Walk with this one at this important time as you might walk with him or her in any challenging experience of life. Be yourself! That is the self that each loved one has come to love. Don't expect more or less of yourself simply because you are meeting a death experience. It is in truth no different than any other part of life.

You can never really be separated from one that you have loved, and from whom you have accepted the rare gift of love. Obviously, this loved one's life experience is going to change through this growth experience, and you will be subject to a sense of separation from him. Your life will undoubtedly have to change too, for this is no less a growth experience for you. You will not have the personal, physical touch of the familiar form of this loved one, but you can grow through this and to an even greater degree free yourself from the sense of separation.

Later on we will consider those physical things that need to be done at the passing of a loved one for whom we have responsibility. We will consider the myriad of challenges and questions that will demand our efficient consideration, but now let us deal only with what occurs within us at the death of a loved one.

It should not be difficult for us to move in our thought to a point of thanksgiving in regard to the death of this loved one who has lived a rich and full life. Now, let us understand that it is not being suggested that we should give thanks for death, even though the circumstances of death may very well be a point of release to one who has fulfilled his or her life experience and is ready, even eager, to move on. We are here suggesting that one of the best ways to deal with death is to move to a point of thanksgiving for all that has been accomplished up to this point in the life of this loved one.

I think about my dad. He was a great guy. He died when he was seventy. He had had a number of heart attacks and his passing, though challenging, was not unexpected. He was a super salesman with more friends around the world than you could count. He had been light-heavy-weight boxing champion of the A.E.F. during World War I. He and my mom parented five healthy, happy kids. During the great depression, he was willing to do anything for his family. He was fun; he was a friend.

I can think of all sorts of things for which I am very thankful in regard to my dad. That very consciousness made his death a growing experience for me, one that was not marred by deep sadness or unhappiness. Of course, I would have preferred that he live on in the familiar form that I knew, but since that was not to be, I am so grateful that I was privileged to be his number two son and to have known and loved him. There were lots of times in my young life when he scared the pants off me, and times when I didn't like him because of the painfully high standard that he set for us kids. The interesting thing is that I find it increasingly difficult to recall those times, but when I can, it is with the gratitude of an adult who appreciates to some degree the blessing that was mine in my childhood.

If you are having the occasion to meet the death of such a one, give thanks. Fill your thought, your memory, your very spirit with an awareness of all that was good about the relationship that you shared. It is amazing what this kind of exercise can do for the deep feelings that you are confronted with. My dad specifically said that he did not want any kind of a funeral service after he died. He was almost adamant in his feelings that he didn't want "a lot of people lining up to look at what I left behind." He felt that what he wanted most was to have those nearest and dearest to him gather in his living room overlooking the Pacific Ocean just at sundown, and there to have a drink for him as we watched the sun settle into the ocean. That was always a favorite time to him. It was a deeply happy time for us and had, I am sure, special significance to each one of us in the privacy of our thoughts that evening.

More often than we realize, some of us are confronted with the death of a relative who is near to us only by virtue of family ties. Sometimes people related to us are very unhappy, miserable people, whom we have grown to dislike, even intensely. Way down in the very private depths of our feelings, we may seem almost glad this this one has died. We probably could never admit that to folks in general, particularly at the time of death. What would people think? So we play a role that we assume is expected of us. But still, there is not the link of conscious love with this family member.

Well, when you stop to think about that, it is pretty normal. There are people all around us whom we may not like, in whose presence we would not wish to be. If that is the case, so be it. We have no need to feel remorse just because that one has passed through the experience of life that we call death. It is ludicrous for us to burden ourselves or the deceased with the sham of pretended admiration or closeness.

I remember a good many years ago attending the funeral of a friend of mine, who on numerous occasions had confided to me the unspanable gulf that existed between him and his estranged father. The father had literally kicked him out of their home when he was in his teens. The rejection and contempt that the father felt were demonstrated over and over throughout the years that intervened. Then, on the occasion of the funeral of my friend, the father attended, and in his remorse even tried to climb physically into the casket with the body of his son during the funeral.

There are probably people in your life and in mine whom we don't like. Some of those may very well be members of our family. Just because we are related by birth doesn't necessarily mean that we will personally have any real relationship together as personalities. We can, however, use the occasion of the death of such a one to grow to the point where we can love him or her as a self or soul that is moving on in life's eternal progression of growth. Every human being deserves respect as a human being, regardless of the things that he or she may have done to alienate us personally. Grief can be a great burden, or even a greater burden, when it involves someone from whom we have been estranged. It would be quite natural for us to feel some sense of guilt regarding this relationship that we have not been able to salvage in life. To bear that kind of emotional burden will serve no useful purpose for us or for the deceased.

Let your evolving philosophy of life and death release this departed one from any bondage of negative emotion. Loose him and let him go. Of course, we all would wish that we could have had a better relationship with any person, but let us not complicate the death experience for ourself or the other by creating a bond of remorse or non-forgiveness.

After all the formalities are over, the funeral is behind you and the estate has been settled, after the initial shock has worn off, there will probably be a continuing process of releasing. The same emotions that you experienced at the point of death will need to be dealt with. Your resolve to deal positively will need to be reinforced to a decreasing extent as time goes by. Time is a healer of all hurts. Be patient with yourself and with those around you. Each time the emotion, be it sadness or remorse, comes to the surface of your thoughts, deal with it head on. Don't be afraid or ashamed to cry, for tears can serve to cleanse and purify your thought and feeling. Reaffirm your faith in the continuity of life and the assurance that every experience in life is a growth opportunity.

There is no place for sadness in the soul that knows, or is seeking to know, that life goes on and that there is no real separation where there is love. You can love enough to grow and let a dying or dead person grow. Death doesn't stop growth; it is, as Dr. Kubler-Ross says, the final stage of growth. The final stage of growth is, after all, the first stage of growth on the next plane of life, whatever that may be.

CHAPTER XI

Dealing With Death of Children

Death is particularly challenging when it involves an infant or a child or a relatively young person. A part of the comparative process in evaluation by which we judge the worth or value of the life experience is the assumption that life is constituted of at least "three score and ten" years of life. Anyone who does not seem to get his fair share of time in this life experience is presumed to have been cheated. This assumption is understandable, particularly in view of the mistaken belief that all there is to life is that which lies between birth and death.

If, as we have postulated, life is an eternal and continuing process, then the validity of this assumption begins to wane. Surely longevity is not the only criterion for evaluating the worth of a life. We have no way at this point of knowing what lies beyond this life experience except that our expanding consciousness of faith, along with our reasonable philosophy of life, can give us the assurance that it will be freed to some degree from the limitations that we continue to impose upon ourselves in this three-dimensional life experience. There is a wisdom, a knowing, an order and rightness that shapes the destinies of all of us, even of those who may not in this experience have evidenced the kind or degree of growth that we have.

It is not impossible for us to know what kind of learning experience the soul or self of our child has come into this life experience to have. As a part of our evolving, reasonable philosophy of life, we have seen that each soul or self chooses the particular life experience into which he enters. He draws to him those associates and those particular aspects of the three-dimensional life that can provide the growth opportunity he requires. He comes also into that environmental situation that requires the particular contributions to growth that he can provide.

The mistake that we so often make is one of limited judgmental evaluation based solely upon the hours or days or months or years that have passed between the birth and death of our child. This is so unfair! That child is an eternal soul who came through us for this experience. He is an eternal soul or self which has had . . . and shall continue to have the opportunities for growth that are eternal life. Kahlil Gibran, in his masterpiece *The Prophet* has put it magnificently, "Your children are not your children. They are the sons and daughters of Life's longing for itself. They come through you but not from you, and though they are with you yet they belong not to you."

One factor that makes it difficult to deal with the death of a relatively young person, particularly one with whom we are closely associated, is the natural, human sense of possessiveness that we feel toward our children. Because a child comes through us physically, and because a child for so many years is so greatly dependent upon us, it is most understandable that we tend to possess him. There is a natural process through which we pass to bring us to the point where we can release our children to be the individuals they are and have always been, even though we have thought of them as ours, or at least as extensions of us. If that process is interrupted, then a whole new dimension is added to the adjustment that we have to make in their death.

Parenthood precludes a sense of responsibility toward our children that often expresses itself in an attitude of possessiveness. Our children become just that—*our* children. In addition to the feeling of loss of a loved one, there is the wrenching experience of having had a possession of our very own taken away from us. The normal process of releasing a child of ours takes a considerable period of time. When we accept the privilege of parenthood, we accept also the responsibility that goes with it.

Too often, young parents are not truly cognizant of the kind of commitment that they are letting themselves in for in the natural act of bearing children. One child demands a commitment of at least eighteen to twenty years. Two children three or four years apart will run that definite commitment up to twenty-four or twenty-five years. A third child can increase that commitment to more than thirty years.

It is no small act on our part when we venture into parenthood. The lives of those children are not dependent only upon us as parents. Each soul or self comes into our experience only partially because of us. There are phases in the life of our children over which we have little or no control. We can only do the best we know how in caring for our children, and to a certain extent we will have to trust in our positive expectancy, or faith, and our reasonable philosophy of life, to carry us through the normal challenges of parenthood.

As our children grow in stature and in wisdom we begin the process of release. When a child can walk, we no longer carry him. When he shows he can reason for himself, we stop thinking for him. When the lad can drive for himself, we can close down the family taxi service. Every parent recognizes that the loosing and letting go of our children is a difficult and often painful process. We all know parents of grown children who have never managed to cut "the apron strings" and let their children become the self-sufficient beings that they are, or should be capable of being. Normally speaking, parents do, because they must, release their children somewhere in the early twenties, and the process of growth and evolution goes on.

When this normal process of release is interrupted by the death of a child, we have a considerable challenge to handle. The process of the application of our philosophy of life and death to the challenge is basically the same, but we have to deal with the additional challenge of having been frustrated in the fulfillment of our sense of responsibility to our child and the disruption of the normal process of release of that loved one. Let us follow the process of the application of our reasonable philosophy of life and death from that point where it seems that there is a fairly immediate probability that death will occur, right on through to our inevitable release and return into the flow of life without the physical presence of this loved one.

If our evolving philosophy of life and death, as we have considered it here, has any validity at all, it should give us some very specific guidelines by which to function. To begin with, let us remember that every soul or self is an eternal entity busy in the process of having those growth experiences that will produce an eternal dominion and authority. What we observe as the limited time, space and experience span of our ailing child, is but an infinitesimally small part of his eternal life experience. Your child or mine has access to the same wisdom or knowing that we have. There is an intelligence that instructs each one of us in the form of interest, desire to accomplish or to be, an intuitive knowing that instructs us to move, to stop, to turn, to act, or to refrain from acting.

Consciously we think and feel and we look around our world for those signs of direction to confirm our inward movement. We think that it is the outer world that has motivated us or caused our movement, but that is not the case. There is, there has to be, an intelligence that directs us from within. We are not usually conscious of this directive force that we have within, because we have limited ourselves to a three-dimensional perspective; nonetheless it is there. Within you and me, and within our children, regardless of their age, experience or lack of experience, there is a knowing that provides the know-how, the direction for us to have those experiences that are appropriate for our growth.

As parents, we tend to burden the self or soul of our children with fear and doubt and uncertainty. This negativity tends to "jam" the reception of their innate guidance. Our evolving faith and understanding should assist us in releasing our child into the wise and loving care of this innate knowing in him. Our love would prompt us to wish that we could meet the challenge in the place of our child, but that cannot be. We must give our child the freedom to meet that which is his to meet, and sustain him in faith and knowing.

For the one whose child seems destined to meet the experience of life that we call death, there is a great responsibility that must not be avoided. In addition to accepting our usual responsibility for the best care that we can provide in a physical way, we have an unavoidable responsibility to provide the love and faith to our child that will strengthen him in meeting his challenge. Just because a child, regardless of age, is meeting the death experience does not relieve us of the responsibility to be the kind of support and lend the kind of love and faith that he needs in this experience, no matter how painful it may be for us.

The parent of what the world calls a terminally ill child has a tremendous responsibility to surround that child with feelings of love and peace and faith. Often we make the mistake of assuming the child does not understand what he is meeting. Perhaps in the conscious sense he does not . . . but the soul or self of him is the one meeting the challenge and is responsive to our every feeling, word, and action. Let us not clog his link with infinite intelligence with our fear and sadness. Instead, immerse him in a constant bath of hope and faith, peace and light. You as a parent were drawn into his life and experience just as much as he was drawn into yours. Our grief can be assuaged more readily if we can rise to the occasion by being the producer of peace, joy, light, and faith rather than the producer of sadness and remorse and fear.

Our evolving, reasonable philosophy of life can be a tremendous blessing to others. Among my dearest friends is a couple who a number of years ago went through the challenge of the death of their youngest child in a drowning accident. They are what the world would call ideal parents, in that they have always had a very close, loving relationship with their children. When their baby, not closely enough tended by a babysitter, crawled to the swimming pool and fell in, the consequences could have had a shattering effect upon the parents and the older brothers and sister. They didn't, however, because of a substantial faith and a remarkable understanding of the continuity of life on the part of the parents. They surely fulfilled all the necessary functions in meeting this experience, but they immediately turned their attention to their older children and to one another.

That little soul moved on unfettered by negative emotions. These wise and loving parents didn't love the child any less in meeting the experience as a great opportunity to grow and to be a part of the growth process of all those around them. Theirs was a great tribute to a soul or self that was and ever shall be a significant part of their eternal lives. I am deeply grateful for the privilege of even just knowing such people.

CHAPTER XII

Dealing With Death
Through Suicide

The phone rang at mid-morning. A local mortician was on the line. He and I worked together on the Mayor's Committee on Alcoholism in our community. He asked if I could come over to an address in the south part of town. I knew he wouldn't ask if it weren't important. The address was of a defunct garage that hadn't been used in some time. Some children playing in the vicinity had looked in a high window at the rear and had reported that there was someone lying on the floor inside. This was reported to the police and then the mortician was called.

The body was that of a friend of mine who apparently had been playing "russian roulette" with a revolver a couple of days earlier. My friend was in his late thirties or early forties. We had worked closely together for some time. He had been given up as a hopeless alcoholic by a lot of people. I felt that we had made a good bit of progress up to this time, but then he had committed suicide.

In all of the serious, conscientious discussions we had had in the many months prior to his suicide, he had threatened many times to take his own life. I felt pretty comfortable with that because I really believed that old wives' tale that people who talk about suicide seldom if ever take their own lives. If anyone tells you that, don't believe them. If anyone ever talks to you about suicide, he is crying out for help. Believe me, there is no platitudinous rule about whether one is the type . . . anybody is the type! Virtually everyone at one time or another has considered suicide. Fortunately, most of us don't give in to such an idea very readily because the instinct of self-preservation is very strong in the vast majority of people, most of the time.

In our death-denying society, suicide presents some very serious challenges to the family and friends that are left behind. When one is confronted with suicide, one experiences a complex mixture of emotions, such as grief, remorse, anger, hurt, frustration and fear. That is quite a load! The very normal response of grief at the loss of a loved one in a very sudden manner tries the faith and understanding of the most stable of us.

When death occurs unexpectedly, we are caught with our defenses down. This could happen at any time and is therefore reason enough for us to deal with the idea of death when we are not under the pressure of death as a fact. It can be a very constructive exercise to deal with death as an idea so that in the event that we are confronted with it as a totally unexpected fact, we will be able to respond effectively.

To the extent that we are able to establish ourselves in a trusting philosophy of life and death, we should be able to handle a sudden death without too much difficulty, because there are no alternatives and it is done. In the event that the sudden death is a suicide, we have the additional burden of vicarious guilt and remorse; and our society has built into us a very strong sense of judgment regarding the act of suicide.

For the benefit of this consideration, let us at least for the moment, set aside our pre-conceptions regarding suicide. Let us, as best we can, be open and receptive to a consideration of suicide in the light of our evolving philosophy regarding life and death. Let us remind ourselves of the reasonable conclusions that we have come to consider, the very reasonableness of which can strengthen us in meeting death wherever, whenever, and however it may come in our world. That philosophy, coupled with an expectancy or faith, is even now enabling us to prepare for our own death experience by living our life more fully here and now.

We have considered that life is not circumscribed by birth and death, but rather that that eternal part of us, our self or our soul, is an eternal entity. We have reasoned that there is no such thing as the cessation of life, there is only a continuing process of which we are all a part. We have seen growth toward ever increasing dominion and authority as the primal cause and purpose of our experience. Surely we have come to conceive that a part of the aim of this growth process is unification with all there is, for in truth, there really is no such thing as separation. Now, remember that we cannot prove or disprove any of this. We are simply seeking a reasonable philosophy that will aid us in our overcoming of the fear that is so much a part of our human experience.

If suicide itself is bad or wrong or evil or a sin, then all of us, saint and sinner are guilty. If you stop and think about it in the light of our evolving philosophy, all of us, in a sense, commit suicide; that is, we cause our physical demise. Most of us do not cause it suddenly by a sudden stop at the end of a long fall or the squeeze of a trigger or the numbness of an overdose, but we still cause our own physical demise. It may take us seventy or eighty or more years, but somehow the responsibility is ours. At the outset of our consideration of suicide, let us make an effort to free ourselves and those who choose to take their own lives from the crushing burden of guilt. Suicide isn't good or bad; it is simply a fact of human experience that is born of our ignorance of the true meaning of life and of our part in it.

One who chooses suicide as a part of his life experience accomplishes only one thing—the postponement of the act of learning whatever life's experience is seeking to teach him. At least, that is the highest and best judgment that we have at this point in our evolutionary process. This act must be a part of the growth process that the self or soul has chosen. Most people will find it difficult to be able to grasp or accept this logic because of the eons of programming that we have subjected ourselves to through our not knowing, but an acceptance of it can set us free from the deep sense of guilt and remorse that we are apt to feel at the suicide of one close to us. Our acceptance can also be a tremendous release to that one who has gone on so suddenly to another plane of being.

Anger, hurt, and frustration also often accompany the normal shock of grief that results from the suicide of one near or dear to us. Here again, these emotions that are added to the normal sense of separation are the direct result of our having been judgmental, individually and culturally, regarding the act of suicide. Because we have culturally felt that suicide is bad, a cop-out, the act of a quitter or weakling, we feel disappointed that someone, with whom we will be judged by association, has let us down.

I recall talking with the mother of a young adult suicide whose most strongly expressed emotion was "how could she do this to us?" There must be a great strength of purpose on our part to release the one who commits suicide. We must, in the light of our evolving philosophy of life and death, loose him and let him go. A suicide, no matter how close he may be to us, hasn't done anything *to us* . . . he has made a choice regarding himself. How we respond to a suicide is our responsibility, not that of the one who has gone on.

We may very well feel a strong sense of fear at the suicide of one near or dear to us, fear for that loved one and fear for ourself. We might feel fear for ourself because of the possibility of suicide on our part in a moment of weakness or extreme distress. It seems logical that the greatest deterrent to suicide is a healthy philosophy of life and death. If we come to understand the true continuity of life, we shall come to realize that we cannot really "cop out" . . . we can only postpone meeting the challenge to growth that we have drawn. It will help us to realize that life is not responsible for our experience, other people are not responsible, neither luck nor chance nor circumstances are responsible . . . we are! If we allow others, any others—persons or circumstances—to provide those conditions through which we may grow, it is still our allowing that has brought us to the point where we can or we must grow. A realistic attitude toward suicide, instead of a judgmental one, can do more than anything else to release us from fear of suicide as a threat to us or to others.

Many people fear for the suicide in the belief that suicide eliminates any other alternatives for him. The threat or danger of some sort of damnation for the suicide is very real in our death-denying culture. If, as we have postulated, life is *the* reality and it is ever evolving, ever expanding reality that produces through growth an ever greater dominion and authority to the self or soul of us, then there truly cannot be a lasting or permanent avoidance of the process.

It would seem that we can learn our lessons that produce growth easily or painfully. We can learn because conditions thrust the growth upon us, or we can learn because we logically and trustingly choose to do so. There are always these options, but the decision is up to us. There are no finalities in life; there are just new beginnings. As the popular song says, "today is the first day of the rest of your life." The thing for us to remember, though, is that it is an eternal life that we are living.

CHAPTER XIII

Dealing With Death
Through Murder

The major cities in the United States are experiencing a terrifying increase in violent crimes. We have come to the point where we seem to accept the fact that it isn't really safe to walk on the street alone at night. There are all kinds of excuses that we give for this change in our social system. Urbanization would certainly appear to be a major contributing factor. For the majority of people living in urban areas, qualitative standards of living have increased considerably. The increased incidence of drug abuse surely can be seen to be a contributing factor to the rise in violence among us. The eternal conflict between the "haves" and the "have nots" must accept a considerable share of responsibility for violent crime as well.

It is interesting to note, though, that the majority of murders in our society today are classed as crimes of passion and are committed by persons known by the victims. More often than we would like to admit, our inability to deal with the complexities of human relationships can end in violence, manslaughter and murder. Such incidents are not, however, limited to urban areas. A considerable number of crimes of passion occur in suburban and rural areas as well. In the majority of cases, murder is committed because of the conflicts between people, and cannot wholly be attributed to their whereabouts.

I live in a small midwestern town of less than twenty thousand population. Several years ago I returned home from a holiday weekend with my teenage daughter. We turned on the television and heard of a local murder that occurred during our absence. The victim was an honors student from our local high school. Her partially clad body had been found in a nearby lake tied with bailing wire. She was a friend of my daughter. The two had worked together on Saturdays at a local store.

The effect of this tragedy on our community as a whole, and on my daughter specifically, was very traumatic. Why? How could such a thing happen? If there is a God, where was he in this youngster's moment of need? The prime suspect in this case was another honors student from the same senior class. The two had been going steady for at least a couple of years. The young man just disappeared once the body was found. Even though the victim was found to have been three or four months pregnant, a girl cannot accomplish that on her own. Where is the justice? How could such a thing happen?

Because of our closeness, there were hours of discussion between my daughter and myself in regard to this tragic experience. A sixteen-year-old girl with a very strong feeling nature will, in circumstances such as this, ask question after question until there is some kind of logical answer forthcoming. The questions that are asked are perfectly fair and demand some kind of reasonable response. If our reasonable philosophy of life and death has any validity, it must be able to be of assistance to us in finding some meaningful answers to the questions that quite naturally arise in the event of murder in general, but more importantly, those that arise in the event of murder of someone close to us.

If, as we have postulated in the development of our reasonable philosophy of life and death, the soul or self of us chooses those experiences in which and through which we can grow and those in and through which we can assist others to grow, then it follows that the soul or self of us has placed us in a position to be a part of this kind of experience. All of the lifetimes of programming that have gone into the development of our race consciousness will resist this idea because of the need we have to compete within our sense of separation one from the other. The whole concept of fairness or unfairness cries out in disagreement when it is suggested that the "innocent" victim of murder might in some way bear a responsibility for the experience.

Before we deal with this matter of responsibility, let us first clarify that we are not here dealing with human or personal responsibility as would be generally understood. In the case of the youngster from our town, we are not suggesting that in comparison to the boy, if in fact the boy committed the murder, she must accept some of the responsibility in a human or personal sense. We are not suggesting that because she was pregnant it would naturally follow that she must share in the responsibility for the violence that resulted in her death. There are those who might suggest that God or fate or some other balancing power had served up her just desserts.

We are here not interested in entering into a discussion of the morality of murder or the morality of whatever circumstances may have led up to such a humanly tragic event. We are here interested in dealing with one soul or self, not the inter-relationships that the soul or self may have had with others. From a human standpoint, we can regret the event and conclude that the "innocent" victim of murder is indeed innocent. We can, if we choose, give in to the very human need to be judgmental in regard to the perpetrator of such a crime. It is perfectly clear that if we do so, we are going to cloud the issue and have increasing difficulty in finding appropriate answers from our evolving reasonable philosophy of life and death that will bring some degree of comfort and understanding by which to deal constructively with this event.

Now let us restate in yet another way one of the basic concepts that we have considered as a reasonable postulate for our reasonable philosophy of life and death. The soul or self of us is an eternal entity. It functions in a universe that is based upon principle. It is not subject to whim or caprice, not of others or of gods or of fate. The soul or self of us is moving eternally from experience to experience to meet those opportunities for growth that are fitting to us in order that we might move progressively toward ever greater and greater degrees of dominion and authority.

It follows then that the soul or self of us is a responsible entity, even though in a limited sense it might appear not to have control over experiences to which it is subject on a human or personal level. Within the tight turn of the river of life in which we find ourselves, it may clearly appear, as we look back to the last bend in the river and forward to the next one, that this experience of murder of a humanly innocent person is without reason or logic; but if we could rise up once more and see the broader picture of the life of such a one, our entire perspective would alter.

A part of the greater or broader perspective would surely reveal that the eternal soul or self of us indeed bears responsibility for the experience. More than that, it would reveal that the eternal soul or self of us has selected this experience, and the other "actors" in the drama, for its own growth, with the full realization that the others concerned are equally involved in a learning experience as well. In the Bhagavad Gita, holy writ for millions of Hindus, the Lord Krishna instructs his student Arjuna in these words, regarding one who is slain: "never is it born nor does it die; never did it come to be nor will it ever come not to be: Unborn, eternal, everlasting is this primordial (self). It is not slain when the body is slain." The suggestion is clear that both he who thinks he kills and he who thinks he can be killed are in error.

The great sense of injustice that we feel and that others very naturally thrust upon us upon the occasion of murder, is extremely difficult to deal with. After all, it is reasonable and logical within the limitations of the three-dimensional realm in which we function. If we would make the most of this opportunity to grow, we must not only release the loved one who has been the victim of murder, but the perpetrator as well. You see, the great opportunity that we have for growth lies in how we deal inwardly with the experience. We have no right to bind our departed loved one with feelings of anguish and bitterness and condemnation. We have no right to heap upon another the negative feelings of condemnation and bitterness and unforgiveness that are born of judgmental thought, for to do so will only burden our soul or self to meet again and again those experiences that provide us with the opportunity to come to know that every soul is free and is moving irresistibly toward its own dominion and authority.

Your loved one who has been the victim of murder or the perpetrator of murder is fulfilling his or her own destiny. The perpetrator must, of course, be subject to the laws of our land, and as a result might even have to experience death quickly or otherwise pay the fine levied by our society for such an act. Every experience, however, is part of an unfolding pattern destined for each one, by each one. We cannot be expected to fully understand all that is involved, because we continue in our journey down the river of life, being limited in how far we can see ahead of us or behind us. We can, however, accept the strengthening faith that there is logic and reason, there is still the outworking of principle even though we may not be able to explain it satisfactorily to ourselves, let alone to others. Loose your loved one, let him go. Know steadfastly that even though death has come violently, and to a human sense unfairly, the words of James Dillet Freeman in his poem "The Traveller" are true:

> He has put on invisibility.
> Dear Lord, I cannot see--
> But this I know, although the road ascends
> And passes from my sight,
> That there will be no night;
>
> That you will take him gently by the hand
> And lead him on
> Along the road of life that never ends,
> And he will find it is not death but dawn.
> I do not doubt that You are there as here,
> And You will hold him dear.
>
> Our life did not begin with birth,
> It is not of the earth;
> And this that we call death, it is no more
> Than the opening and closing of a door--
> And in Your house how many rooms must be
> Beyond this one where we rest momently.
>
> Dear Lord, I thank You for the faith that frees,
> The love that knows it cannot lose its own;
> The love that, looking through the shadows, sees
> That You and he and I are ever one!

CHAPTER XIV

The Logistics of Death

Our society becomes increasingly complex with the passage of every year. Our communities, our states, and our federal government continue to pass laws that affect each of us. At the death of a loved one we are literally swamped with decisions to be made, forms to be filled out and filed. There may be a will to be dealt with, the insurance policies to be submitted for payment, and the registration of the death certificate to be seen to. There may be the need of a request for a post mortem.

What kind of final arrangements are appropriate? If pre-arrangements haven't been made, there will be need for the procurement of a burial plot, once the decision has been made to bury the remains of our loved one. If that is the decision, what type of coffin or casket should be selected? An increasing number of people are choosing to cremate rather than bury, and if that is the decision, will arrangements be made for the scattering of the ashes or should a suitable niche be purchased? If so, will there be some kind of identification there?

Someone has to accept responsibility for the personal belongings of our loved one. There is always the question of property rights, and it is important to be sure that we conform to the laws concerning these rights. Because we live in an increasingly materialistic society, even the people we love and who love us can become difficult when the time comes for the distribution or disposal of the possessions of a loved one.

Faced with all of these questions, there is often the complication of the uncertainty of whose responsibility it is to find the appropriate answers. When there are several members of a family who must be consulted, it has to be recognized that each one is being affected by the experience according to his or her own emotional state and degree of understanding. Probably, no two of us will respond in just the same way, to the same degree.

For the majority of us there are some religious attitudes or opinions that demand consideration. For example, there are many people whose religious bias makes it impossible for them to seriously consider cremation. There are those of us who feel that a specific ritual of our church or synagogue is mandatory for the occasion of the death of a loved one. The rites of our church or synagogue or those of our loved one must be taken into consideration, and if ours differ from those of our deceased loved one's, we may very well be confronted with additional emotional complications.

With all of the questions, the demands, the requirements that we are called upon to deal with, it is no surprise that the death of a loved one can be a very traumatic experience. A part of our reasonable philosophy about life and death must surely be that life never demands more of us than we are able to cope with. For every question there is an answer, for every challenge there is a solution.

It is important to hold to this attitude so that we can logically, calmly and considerately accomplish all of those things that need to be done by us. One of the finest tributes that can be paid to a loved one who has died is to love and care enough to deal with him or her in death as we would in any other part of the life experience. Just relax, there is a world of caring that is eager to be of assistance. You are never all alone unless you choose to be.

Who are they who care enough to be of assistance in your hour of need? There may be any or all of the following: close friends who care for you, your loved one's doctor and medical staff, a mortician and his entire staff, an attorney, an insurance agent, an accountant or bookkeeper, a clergyman, and probably a host of others that I haven't even thought of. The world is peopled with individuals who want to be needed, people who will be grateful for the opportunity to help. Your experiences in life may not have assured you of this truth, but if you need, and you are willing to reveal that need, it is possible that you can be a real blessing to others in your hour of need.

It is well to remember that with the possible exception of the professionally qualified persons to whom you might reach out, most people have as much difficulty dealing effectively with another's grief as you have. It is not necessary to impress others with the depth or extent of your grief or your love for your deceased loved one. It is unreasonable, therefore unfair, to assume that others will feel the way or the extent to which you feel at the passing of your loved one.

Life on the human level is made up to a tremendous degree of the sharing of who and what we are with others and of partaking of that same sharing with others. None of us can live in a vacuum. We need each other! Out of that need that is common to all of us, we have created friendships that are among our most precious possessions. Often our friends are not physically near to assist us in our time of need, and often they are. Such a one can be of the greatest assistance in dealing with the complexities of demands, questions and requirements at the passing of a loved one. If our life is important enough to share with a loved one or friend . . . death, and possibly grief as a part of life, is a precious possession too, that we should be willing to share with another.

If you are blessed with a friend nearby, share your experience with him or her. The sharing can be a precious thing to both of you. Often a friend may not be any better equipped to find answers to questions and fulfill requirements than you are, but you will find that love expressed in a look, the firm handclasp of assurance of sharing can be a tremendous blessing and support. Sustaining strength and support do not have to come through knowing all the answers, speaking all the words, or fulfilling all the requirements.

Often in the death of a loved one there is a doctor or a nurse who has shared in this part of life's experience that we call death. Though there are great demands put upon these professionals, it is important to remember that first and foremost they are people. Generally speaking, they are folks who care and want to help, or they wouldn't be professionally involved in the healing arts. Because they are professionally involved, however, does not necessarily preclude that they also have their emotional and mental problems with death, dying, and grief. Simply by virtue of their more frequent exposure to death and their repeated experience in relationship with those meeting bereavement, they can be a valuable source of light and guidance to us as we meet the crisis of the death of a loved one. Behind the professional, efficient exterior of every professional medical person, there lurks a warm, caring, human being. Let's program ourselves to the anticipation of a breakthrough to such a one.

An increasing number of people are choosing to leave their body to medical research. In that event, which is certainly laudable, and an evidence of an unconscious if not conscious realization that we are more than, and therefore transcend, the body, we would not have the occasion of coming in contact with a mortician or funeral director. For most of us, however, this one person can be of the greatest possible assistance. A mortician probably knows more of the answers to the questions and challenges arising out of the death of a loved one than anyone else. Your mortician has access to information regarding the laws with which we must deal, he usually is a retailer of coffins and caskets, and is regularly in communication with cemeteries, crematoriums, gravestone masons, etc.

A good professional mortician can be our very best friend in this time of need. Like in any other area of human experience, most morticians or funeral directors are honest, caring, considerate human beings who are motivated in some degree to helping people. It is important to bear in mind that we are usually pretty vulnerable while in the midst of bereavement because of our emotions, and therefore could easily exceed our means in an unrealistic attempt to pay tribute to our loved one. Most funeral directors would not knowingly so motivate us, but then there are those whose own needs or greeds might overshadow their concern for us. It might be well for us to have others with us as we enter into our negotiations with the funeral director.

Your funeral director is prepared to obtain the body of your loved one from the hospital or home and undertake all or any of the services that are necessary to prepare that body for burial or cremation. These services can be minimal or extremely extensive. They can include embalming, cosmetics, and even a degree of what might be termed "plastic surgery" in an attempt to give the appearance of life as the loved one expressed or manifested it in life. They could include dressing the deceased and placing the body for display or disposal. For those who have no church or synagogue preference, your funeral director can obtain the services of a suitable clergyman for you. Almost all funeral directors can be of assistance in the fulfilling of all the details involved in the physical disposition of the body of your loved one.

If there are many fiscal complexities involved in the estate of a loved one, it is generally wise to obtain the services of an attorney. The need for legal counsel is becoming more and more necessary as our society becomes increasingly complex. The vast majority of lawyers are honest, concerned and committed human beings who are motivated by a desire to serve people. Here again, this is evidenced by the very act of following this profession. If you do not have an attorney, information regarding one can be obtained from your local Bar Association.

Most people today carry some kind of insurance. Hopefully, each of us who is consciously seeking to develop a reasonable philosophy of life and death will assure that any policies that we may have on our life or the life of one with whom we live will be retained in a logical place for easy recovery when needed. Any committed, professional insurance agent will be eager to assist you or me at that time when we have questions regarding insurance when a loved one has died. Like doctors and nurses, lawyers and funeral directors, an insurance agent is one motivated to a certain degree to helping people.

It may be necessary at the demise of a loved one to obtain the services of an accountant or bookkeeper, but probably only if the estate required such services on a more or less regular basis before death. The larger and more complex an estate, the greater the likelihood that accounting services would be required. There are all sorts of accounting firms, accountants, bookkeeping businesses and bookkeepers around. If the need should arise, your banker, your attorney, or a friend can help in guiding you to a helpful person.

In the bumper sticker craze there are all sorts of admonitions and slogans. One that I saw once read, "If all else fails, try God." To many, this is more than just an admonition or slogan . . . it is a way of life. To the reader who has a religious affiliation, even if it is only serving him at birth, marriage, and death specific guidance regarding the selection of a clergyman is not needed. Those who have religious affiliation or involvement already know the kind of help that a clergyman can provide at a time of bereavement. To those who have, for whatever reason, no acquaintance with a clergyman, the occasion of the death of a loved one can be a marvelous opportunity to transcend our prejudices regarding formalized religion and the professionals who espouse that religion.

As in any other field, there are those in the religious field whose motivation at a time of bereavement is highly suspect. I know of a small-town clergyman who had little if any help to offer during the period of the terminal illness, only to become offensive to the family when he was not invited to conduct the funeral service. Unfortunately, his motivation was clearly the possible stipend that would be forthcoming for conducting such a service.

There are many clergymen whose primary motivation is to utilize the occasion of a funeral to expose the captive audience to their particular dogmatic view-point without regard for the feelings of the bereaved. I'm sure that you might have had the experience of attending the funeral service of one whose life exemplified generosity, love, and kindliness only to be exposed to a tirade of "hell-fire and damnation" by a clergyman. At the other extreme, there are those who are so unrelated to reality that they prove an embarrassment to the family.

Perhaps you have heard one of the many variations of the story of the evil, hard-nosed, inconsiderate and blasphemous man who died. The day came for the funeral and the haggard widow and her children were seated at the front of the funeral chapel. The "sweet and light" clergyman went on and on about "our dearly beloved who has left us so bereft," and finally the widow nudged her eldest son seated beside her and said, "Maybe you better go up there and look in that box and see if it's your Pa."

Unquestionably, the vast majority of clergymen are those who are well equipped to be of tremendous blessing to the bereaved. For most of us, the trauma of meeting the death of a loved one is pretty staggering. We seem at this moment of extreme vulnerability to be a hodge-podge of opinions and emotions, prejudices and fears, doubts and uncertainties. Nothing seems to make much sense. A clergyman with counseling skills can be a tremendous blessing in sorting things out. Compassion and caring characterize the committed clergyman. If he were not so committed, he would never have been motivated to become a minister or continue to be one. For most of us, the vastness of our not knowing becomes so evident in bereavement that this occasion can afford us the opportunity to experience inward growth as at no other time in our experience. A clergyman can be of inestimable help if only we can bring ourselves to reach out for help.

There is far more caring in the hearts of people than we generally realize. In our time of challenge in meeting the death of a loved one, we have a splendid opportunity to touch this caring and find blessings that can sustain and strengthen us all the rest of our eternal life. Think how wonderful it will be to be able to share the awareness of that caring with others so that they will be able to meet similar challenges more effectively in their lives. Wouldn't it be great if we could all come to know that through our unity we can share the caring for each other?

CHAPTER XV

Ever and Always One

Because you and I are capable of a tremendous sense of attachment to those whom we love, people who have loved and strengthened and blessed us, we all have a great need to be strengthened in some sort of knowing continuity of relationship with those who have preceded us in death. The most frequently asked question at the time of the death of a loved one is, "Will we meet again?" Our sense of attachment produces a great void, that at times feels as though it can never be filled. It is often so great that it becomes a physical hurt. It has often been the direct cause of even the death of the bereaved one. Many who have had to meet the death of a loved one without a reasonable philosophy of life and death, have felt that they simply could not make the adjustment without the assurance that we will meet again.

Let us be comforted, we will meet again! We can never ever be truly separated from one whom we have loved. If at this point in your life you have some difficulty in grasping the intellectual rationality that we have shared in our attempts to evolve a reasonable philosophy of life and death, don't fight it. Just let go, know that in an intelligent universe such as ours, there is reason and logic and somehow, in some way you will be reunited with your loved ones.

It isn't necesary for you to be able to understand, if understanding is difficult in the midst of your deep emotions regarding the death of your loved one. Just accept that anything as beautiful as your love for that person and the love that has been returned to you, will not be lost. Be patient, look forward eagerly to that time and that place in which there will be the reuniting of all that you are with those who have gone on.

It may be difficult for you to think in any other terms than those that confine your loved one by a name and a face and a personality that you have come to know and love. If the concept of life beyond this life in an eternal progression is one that is frightening or confusing, let it go; don't be concerned. You may very well need to think in terms of a heaven, or you may be able to accept another life in this human form or another plane of existence that defies description, but whatever you do, know that there is no real, forever separation.

Love is a power of mind and heart that functions in a simple and wonderful way. It is that in us that draws us irresistibly to the object of our love and makes us one with him or her. There is a divine kind of chemistry that takes place on the feeling level that unifies us with those whom we love in an even more perfect way than the physical chemistry that occurs when our love brings us to the point of coitus. It makes us a part of one another in an eternal sense. A part of all that we are becomes a part of our loved one through the very love that links us. A part of our loved one becomes an eternal part of us as a divinely natural part of that very love that links us. Perhaps it could be said that on the feeling level, we mate with each one whom we love. That union cannot be severed by this experience that we call death. You and I will always be part and parcel with those whom we have loved and those who have loved us.

Hate is a power of mind and heart that functions in a simple and wondrous way too. Hate is love clad in an unfamiliar garb, but it works in exactly the same way. There is a divine kind of chemistry that takes place on the feeling level that unifies us with those whom we hate. This may be a truth that we don't want to accept, but it certainly seems reasonable that if it is the investment of our feeling nature that makes us eternally one with the objects of our love, then it is the investment of our feeling nature as hate that will surely make us eternally one with the objects of our hate.

Most of our relationships are not purely love or purely hate in a relative sense. Most of our relationships are a mixture of love and hate, just as our lives are a mixture of good and bad, nice and not so nice, negative and positive. In the elemental world, it is the balance of positive and negative that is demonstrated as reality. In our human relationships, there is a constant blending of love and hate, of kindness and meanness, of giving and of receiving.

One of the great truths that our evolving reasonable philosophy of life and death can bring to us is the realization that the choice is ours to purify all of our relationships so that whatever experiences lie before us, they will be a part of our expanding realization of dominion and authority. Now the logical question that arises is one that would seek to define the ultimate dominion and authority. It is not possible for us to be able to define at this point in our evolution just what that ultimate will be, but whatever it will be, if we so decree, it will be good, it will be beautiful and it will be wonderful. Remember, ours is a universe of balance, based upon principles that will increasingly and continually manifest greater and greater order and harmony, greater and greater goodness and beauty. We are the artisans who form and shape our universe according to our expanding consciousness of dominion and authority.

Be grateful that death has come your way, make of it a thing of beauty. Clothe death in the beautiful raiment of life that is eternal. There is great goodness in life and since death is an integral part of life, it too can be beautiful. We are now one, ever and always one with life and with all that there is in life. We have the choice to make it beautiful and fulfilling by our power to decree that it is so. We have the dominion and authority now, and we can live our life in beauty and loveliness.